Rossiter Worthington Raymond

Camp and Cabin

Sketches of life and travel in the West

Rossiter Worthington Raymond

Camp and Cabin

Sketches of life and travel in the West

ISBN/EAN: 9783337097288

Printed in Europe, USA, Canada, Australia, Japan

Cover: Foto ©Andreas Hilbeck / pixelio.de

More available books at **www.hansebooks.com**

CAMP AND CABIN:

SKETCHES OF LIFE AND TRAVEL

IN THE WEST.

By ROSSITER W. RAYMOND,
LATE U. S. COMMISSIONER OF MINING STATISTICS; EDITOR
"ENGINEERING AND MINING JOURNAL;" AUTHOR
"MINES OF THE WEST," ETC.

NEW YORK:
FORDS, HOWARD, & HULBERT.
1880.

COPYRIGHT, 1879,
BY ROSSITER W. RAYMOND.

*Electrotyped and Printed
By Rand, Avery, & Company,
117 Franklin Street,
Boston.*

THE sketches collected in this little volume have been printed in various periodicals within the last eight or nine years; and the reader will bear this in mind as an explanation of the fresh enthusiasm with which some of them speak of scenes not so unfamiliar to the reading public now as when these papers were written. This is particularly true of the "Sketches of the Yellowstone Country," which it was my privilege to traverse in 1871, when few white men had seen its beauties and wonders.

With the single exception of "The Widow Baker," the contents of the book are studies of character and scenery in the Far West. The only justification I can offer for including a New-England story in such a collection is the fact that the language and the influence of New England are found everywhere in the West, and that nobody objects to their company.

R. W. R.

BROOKLYN, N.Y., Dec. 10, 1879.

CONTENTS.

	PAGE
THANKSGIVING JOE	7
AGAMEMNON	47
I. — Young Bullion	47
II. — Further Acquaintance	60
III. — The Prodigal Father	71
IV. — The School-Teacher	81
V. — Not Miss Mary — but "quite Contrairy"	91
VI. — Similia Similibus Curantur	99
WIDOW BAKER	104
I. — Squire and Deacon	104
II. — The Story of the Bakers	110
III. — Board and Lodging	117
IV. — Susan Peabody	124
V. — Jotham	129
VI. — How the Widow Interfered	139
WONDERS OF THE YELLOWSTONE	153
I. — An Exploring Party	153
II. — Up the Madison	162
III. — March and Camp	168
IV. — Hot-Springs and Geysers	177
V. — The Lower Geyser-Basin of the Fire-Hole	186
VI. — The Upper Geyser-Basin of the Fire-Hole	193
VII. — Yellowstone Lake and River	201
THE ICE-CAVES OF WASHINGTON TERRITORY	208
THE ASCENT OF GRAY'S PEAK	225

CAMP AND CABIN.

THANKSGIVING JOE.

A STORY OF THE SAGE-BRUSH.

EXACTLY whereabouts in the State of Nevada lies the now depopulated and abandoned district once known to its numerous residents, and introduced by "The Reese River Reveille" to fame, as Silver Sheen, I shall not reveal, lest some enterprising person should start at once to find it, and to "relocate"—that is to say, "jump"—the extremely valuable claims which some of my friends still own (and hope to sell) within its borders. Suffice it to say, therefore, that Silver Sheen was somewhere between Washoe and White Pine, and partook, in the opinion of its population, of the favorable "indications" of both places. Certainly it looked quite as promising as did either of those famously productive mining-fields before their treasures had been discovered. But, to be candid, so does any point you may please to choose in that vast desert basin known as "the sage-brush country." Everywhere there are the same broad, arid valleys, in which feeble mountain streams lose themselves and disappear without gaining any goal; the same bunch-grass, withered and unpromising, but in reality nutritious, — a sort of standing hay, with seeds like kernels of grain held tightly in its dried-up fingers; the same bare, weather-beaten hills, cleft by precipitous cañons in which are hidden stunted plantations of *piñon* and cottonwood, and along the sides of which, after snows melt in the early summer, innumerable flowers adorn the desolation with a brief glory; the same dust-columns, mysteriously rising in hot afternoons from the surface of the plain, and whirling in slow dances like tall, slender genii of the air; the same exquisite mirage, mocking the traveler with visions of rippling lakes and cool bowery islands, where in reality only the alkali flats stretch away, varied by an occasional clump of gray bushes; the same inevitable, ubiquitous sage-brush, always old, always dusty, always wasting its aromatic fragrance upon heedless breezes or scornful men; the white sage, small and silvery, beloved of cattle; the soft blue sky, the transparent air that brings near the most distant horizon, and makes the day's long journey seem in prospect but an hour's walk; the magical hues of brown and purple that clothe at sunrise and sunset the mountain-side, and the rich golden shade that rests upon the meadows and slopes of bunch-grass: these elements are found in so many localities, that I run no risk of exposing Silver Sheen to the invasion of "jumpers" when I say that it possessed them all.

I am reasonably safe, moreover, in remarking that the district was richly endowed with mineral wealth. Who ever knew of a mining-district in the West that was not? Of course it had a "Mammoth" vein, and a "Eureka," and a "Crown Point No. 2," and a "Ruby," and numerous other promising deposits, carefully baptized with names of good augury. Of course, also, there was a grand tunnel scheme for piercing through the whole mountain-range, and "developing its inexhaustible wealth;" and a stamp-mill (an experimental five-stamp affair) for reducing ores; and of course the ores were refractory, and wouldn't be reduced without some patent process yet undiscovered, but certain to be discovered if "capital" could be had; and of course there was a weekly paper, and a half-dozen bar-rooms, and talk of a church. So far, nobody can distinguish Silver Sheen from many another district in similar circumstances. The driver of a semi-weekly stage which carried the mail from Austin to all these districts in succession could scarcely have told the camps apart, but for his personal acquaintance with the bar-tenders and their beverages, and with the peculiar bad piece of road that each cañon presented.

But Silver Sheen possessed Thanksgiving Joe, and

he was certainly unique. Individual character develops eccentricity much more easily in such rough societies than under the restraints and conventionalities of polite life. All the citizens of Silver Sheen were peculiar, each in his way, and each without attracting special comment upon his oddity. Old Heinrich, who would wear a red bandana in place of a hat; Sam Wetherill, who regularly put on a white shirt and a blue swallow-tail coat with brass buttons every Sunday morning; Redhead Pete, who spent all his earnings in bribing Shoshone Indians to show him the Lost Silver Mine, — a mass of native silver, concerning which everybody knows that it exists, and nobody knows where, — these gentlemen, and a host of others who squandered at poker and monté the proceeds of their labor or their speculations, were allowed to pursue their ways without ridicule, censure, or admiration. Then why should Thanksgiving Joe be regarded as singular?

This singularity could not consist, either, in the mystery that surrounded his previous life. As Col. Gore remarked in a quiet evening gathering at the International, " The past, gentlemen, — I say it without hesitation, and I think no person present will differ : if so, I would like to speak further with that person, — the past belongs to the individooal! It is sacred, gentlemen, sacred ! "

A certain portion of the colonel's past had been spent in sacred seclusion between stone walls; and there were not a few among his auditors who had their own reasons for guarding their own memories. So no questions were asked by anybody, for fear of questions in reply. Every man's career was held to have begun when he first "struck into the sage-brush." For a new district must be populated by the overflow from older ones, and it is the scum which overflows; and if you keep stirring it up, why, nothing will ever settle. I fancy, moreover, that there is in this rude tolerance an element of noble feeling, a germ of charity, a recognition of the duty of giving another chance to those who, " the luck being against them," have fallen from respectability, even so far as the humiliation of public exposure. Certainly I have known some instances of lives once wrecked that were successfully reconstructed, and launched again upon honorable voyages, from the friendly oblivion of such communities.

Yet, after all, Thanksgiving Joe had appeared in Silver Sheen in a manner calculated to distinguish him, even in that adventurous and uninquisitive society. For, as the colonel said to Mr. Pickens of Chicago, when he pointed out to that gentleman, the morning after his arrival, the cabin of Thanksgiving Joe, high up the cañon, half a mile beyond any other, " He never came to Silver Sheen at all, sir: Silver Sheen came to him. When our hardy pioneers first entered this secluded but immensely endowed region, and penetrated to the heart of its argentiferous belt, there, sir, prostrate upon the outcrop of the biggest quartz-ledge in the camp, they found him lying, with a bullet in his shoulder, and — and a fever in his brain," added the colonel, to satisfy his ear for rhetoric.

This had, in truth, been the introduction of Joe's fellow-citizens to him. While he was still unconscious, oscillating between life and death, they had scoured the neighborhood to find the villain who had shot him. It must have been his "pardner;" and the shot had been delivered from behind, — two circumstances which would have secured short shrift for the culprit if he had been caught. But the search was fruitless; and the boys returned from such trivial distractions to the serious work of life. The district had to be organized, and provided with a name. "Murder Cañon" did duty for a few weeks; but when Col. Gore made his appearance it was changed, after an eloquent speech from him, to "Silver Sheen." Then veins had to be discovered, and claims "located," "recorded," and "prospected." Yet Joe was not entirely forgotten. A rough cabin was constructed over the very spot where he had been found: in this the sick man was made rudely comfortable; and, one at a time, the population took turns in watching with him. Moreover, they located in his name, and set apart for him, two hundred feet of the "ledge" on which he had fallen, and "which, gentlemen," said the colonel, "he had recorded with his blood."

All this had happened two years before the time

at which my story is going — by and by — to begin. Joe recovered his consciousness after a week, and his strength in the course of two months. The man who was with him when he first awoke in his right mind, from the critical sleep that denoted the turning of the fever, remarked in describing the scene that he " never see a feller so grateful for nothin' at all. Thanked me for a drink o' water's if it'd been a barrel o' whiskey. Asked me whar he was, 'n I told him; 'n how he came thar, 'n I told him; 'n whether anybody was with him, 'n I told him nary one; 'n I jest informed him what a kiting old hunt we had for the feller as drawed on him f'm behind, 'n how mad we was not to git a holt on him; and says he, ' Thank God!' and goes to sleep again like a baby."

The next man on watch had a few additional particulars to report. The patient had awaked again at midnight, and inquired after a buckskin money-belt, which, having been found by his side apparently empty when he was first discovered, had been kept rather by accident than design, and lay at that moment neglected on the floor in a corner of the cabin. The belt was brought to him; and he lifted it feebly, without any expression of surprise at its lightness, ran his fingers along the pliant leather to the end, and then with a sudden smile said, " Thank God!" and dropped to sleep again. The watcher, unaccustomed to hear such expressions of gratitude from men whose money-belts had been rifled (for this was the universal verdict with regard to Joe's case), had subsequently examined the belt, and found in it a folded paper, bearing these words in a handwriting which might have been that of a woman, — but on this point the witness, being no expert, and a little off practice besides, could not be positive : —

" Let us come before His presence with thanksgiving; "

and below them a date (time but no place being given) and a single initial J. The date was five years old. He had spelled out the motto, and returned the paper to its resting-place, with a half-superstitious feeling that it was an amulet of some sort. A similar impression prevailed among those who heard of it; and from that day the convalescent was called Thanksgiving Joe, a title which he accepted without protest or inquiry. The " Joe " was a happy expansion of the J in the secret paper; and, as the recipient of the name answered when thus addressed, it served all the purposes of a complete and perfect title. To a visitor who once asked him if that were his real name, he replied simply, " It is my given name ;" and curiosity received no further satisfaction.

When Joe got well enough to work, he began as a day-laborer for another miner; for in all the new districts there are almost from the beginning a few at least who bring some money with them, which they can employ in the more rapid development of the claims they select; and by working for these few at high rates of wages the others earn the funds necessary for the purchase of food and clothing to supply them while they lay open their own selected ground. Like all the miners in Silver Sheen, Joe did a good day's work for a day's wages. Laziness was not the besetting sin of the boys, except, perhaps, on occasions when they really laid themselves out to be lazy. Then even Broadway could not turn out an equal number of more perfectly listless and vacuous loafers. At other times that sort of thing was left mainly to Col. Gore, whose business was loafing as a sort of master of ceremonies to the bar-room of the International, in the profits of which he had a share.

But Thanksgiving Joe had his own way of loafing. Nobody was more faithful than he with pick or sledge while the "shift" lasted; but when work was done he would go off up the cañon alone to his solitary cabin, and presently would be seen the slender smoke of his fire as he fried his bacon and boiled his coffee. A little later Joe himself would be visible against the clear yellowing sky, as he sat silent in front of the cabin-door, with his pipe in his mouth, and his hands placidly folded, a picture of rest and contented meditation. In any other state of society he would have been a strange figure. His hair and beard were long and snow-white, his form was slightly bent; but these signs of age were merely the results of his fever, and were moreover contradicted by the brightness of his dark eyes, and the great strength which he occasionally exhibited. When the drift of the Desdemona caved in, and the day-shift were all caught in the timbers, it was Joe who held up the lagging in the broken ground till the boys got a stull wedged under it, and crawled out safe and sound. And when the memorable cloud-burst of '69 took place on the summit above Silver Sheen, and twenty feet of water came booming down the cañon, it was Joe who waded in the nick of time to the shebang where Sam Wetherill lay helpless with rheumatism (the result, by the way, of too much white shirt on an inclement Sunday), and brought him bodily, mattress, vicuña blanket, and all, to the dry bank. In short, Thanksgiving Joe was looked upon by his comrades as a sort of tutelary demi-god, a Hercules or Hiawatha, dwelling somewhat apart, but ready to descend at a moment's notice, and perform deeds of deliverance for the dwellers in the land below.

As they had taken turns watching with him while he was ill, so now they took turns in visiting him; for it was soon discovered that before two or three listeners he was prone to silence, but when a single friend approached him sympathetically he would talk with a simple, homely elevation of spirit that made him seem like a messenger from another country. "He ain't our kind exactly," the boys concluded; "but he's a better kind, and no shenannigan about him either." ("Shenannigan" is the miner's term for humbug.) So they fell into the habit of strolling up the cañon, one at a time, to hear Joe talk.

The nickname they had given him grew more and more appropriate as they learned to know him better; for the characteristic feature of his moods and words was a marvelous perpetual gratitude. "No: he don't look on the bright side neither," replied Sam Wetherill one day, to somebody's comment upon one of Joe's sayings: "things don't have nary bright side nor dark side to him. Told me that himself. Says he, 'When things is transparent, it's bright o' both sides,' says he, 'purvided there's a light on t'other;'" which somewhat distorted version of Joe's apothegm conveyed well enough the meaning that was meant to shine through it.

With his first savings Joe had fitted himself out for a period of labor on his own hook at the Mammoth vein, on which, by common consent, he held the central claim. But the Mammoth, like many another huge quartz outcrop in that country, seemed to consist of a maximum of barren gangue and a minimum of valuable ore. Black specks there were through the mass, and now and then a considerable body of some unknown mineral, over which the most experienced miners shook their heads, and said it was "no doubt this yer base metal, and wouldn't amalgamate worth a red." Joe toiled patiently on, however, until he had sunk his prospecting shaft, without aid from any other person, to the depth of twelve feet, and had extracted from it a dozen tons of rock, out of which a couple of tons of ore were, with much hammering and overhauling, selected. By this time the little five-stamp mill had been erected in the camp; and to this establishment Joe packed a ton of his selected ore, to have it "worked" as a test. In a few days a stylish certificate was returned to him, from which it appeared that his ore had yielded two dollars and fifty cents, while the charge for operating upon it was twenty-five dollars. It took the last coin in his leather belt to pay the bill; but he paid it like a man, and walked straight back to the Desdemona, where they were glad enough to take him again into the day-shift.

That evening Sam Wetherill found him smoking his pipe as usual in front of the cabin. This edifice, by the way, deserves a brief description. It was constructed of piñon (nut-pine) stems, sharpened at the lower end, and driven into the rocky *débris*, which took, in that locality, the place of soil. Three sides of the single apartment constituting the dwelling were thus inclosed. In one of them a door was constructed by the simple process of leaving out three or four stakes. The fourth side, or back, was formed by the projecting outcrop of the "Mammoth Ledge," itself; and Joe, having more room than he needed for his bunk and stool, and the shelf which served him as a table, had carried on his mining operations in the place where he slept and ate, gradually accumulating a heap of waste rock, which he piled up into a heavy partition between the bedroom and the mine. In this way the mine, which began by being in doors, gradually found itself out doors, and caused no further inconvenience to the house than might result from the dropping, after a blast, of a stray rock through the roof. But nobody was inside at such times; and the damage was easily repaired with a little sage-brush and adobe clay, the latter being, in fact, the universally useful material with which all leaks in Silver Sheen were stopped against wind and weather.

It was before this mud-and-stockade villa that Sam Wetherill found Thanksgiving Joe, after his first day of renewed experience in the Desdemona. Sam's way of meeting such a disappointment as he thought Joe had experienced would have been to put on that white shirt and that blue dress-coat, and drown his sorrows in a majestic spree at the International; but, feeling instinctively that this remedy would not suit his friend, he came up to show his sympathy in the way of words at least, not without a shade of secret satisfaction that Joe had finally struck a piece of ill fortune, over which even he could scarcely give thanks.

"A little down on yer luck, old man?" was his condolorous greeting. "Wal now, it was too bad for this yer Mammoth Ledge to go back on yer that way! That thar base metal don't do nothin' in the pans but jest flour the quick, 'n slum it all up.[1] But you jest hold up your head, old man, 'n get a pardner, 'n pros-

---

[1] Granulate the quicksilver used in amalgamation, and render it foul.

pect around a little. 'S no good, this yer coyotin' alone,[1] 'n backin' out o' yer hole every time you want a drink o' water. 'F I hadn't gone in with Dutch Heinrich, on the Bismarck Extension,—almighty big thing too,—I'd like to be yer pardner myself: 'n thar's Redhead Pete, he's a good hand to work, 's long's he *does* work; but he's off agin arter that lost silver mine,—somebody 'll find that thar mine some o' these days; but it won't be Pete. Dutchy says there's no end o' stories about sich mines in his country, and nobody finds 'em on purpose. Some galoot out after jackass-rabbits, or sage-hens, or mountain-sheep, jest accidentally pulls up a bush, or sets down on a rock, 'n happens to look between his boots, 'n thar's a chunk o' the clear bullion 950 fine. But Pete—he'll never find nothin' but Injun wicky-ups.[2] However, *you* won't have no trouble about a pardner. Anybody'll be glad to get *you*, 'n set you up in bacon and beans to start on too. So you jest shake yourself, old man, 'n cheer up. It's all fer the best, you know—'f yer able to see it in that light."

Sam was very well satisfied with the rate at which he was getting on in his new rôle of messenger of consolation; but, as he afterwards expressed it, his "idees all leaked out" of him when Thanksgiving

---

[1] Digging like a coyote, or prairie-fox.
[2] The slight temporary shelter of brush, under which the Nevada Indians sleep, not worthy to be compared with the wigwams and lodges of the stronger and richer tribes of the North.

Joe took his pipe from his mouth, and said reflectively, —

"There isn't any other light, is there?"

"Wal, no," replied Sam in a dubious way, and added, with evident relief, as if he had found a solution, "not ef you see it in *that* light."

"Exactly," continued Joe. "Light is light; and there's only one kind, thank God!"

"An' may I be — if you ain't the" —

(These dashes are not my device for indicating Sam's ready profanity. They show where that fluent blasphemer actually paused and choked, leaving a significant silence. For Joe's thanksgiving carried a sort of echo, in the presence of which a man couldn't start right off, and invoke heaven or hell as if nothing had happened. Moreover, Sam's choking attracted his own attention as a novel phenomenon. He stopped for a moment, pondered it, and "broke out in a new spot" as follows) : —

"The boys in this yer camp mention — Him, you know" — here Sam took off his hat, and replaced it with the air of having done the handsome thing for once in his life — "tol'ble frequent and free; but I don't jest recall any onreas'nable number of 'em as lays 'emselves out to thank him. They ain't heavy on the thank! They jest let the parsons do that by contract, 'n *they* take it mighty easy, — only one shift a week, 'n singlehand drillin' at that. But you do the thankin' fur the crowd. Not that anybody's got any 'bjection; only, when you take to thankin' over them mill-returns, it might sort o' seem to any feller that didn't know yer ways, as if you was p'raps rubbin' it in a trifle,—playing off on us, you know. Now, you can't be glad o' that thar base metal, you know: it's agin reason."

"I didn't say I was glad," replied Joe imperturbably, watching the long shadows from the summit as they reached down like fingers, and clasped the settlement in the cañon. "I am *thankful* now ; and I *expect* to be glad."

Sam seated himself by his paradoxical friend, like one who was bound to get to the bottom of a mystery.

"Go easy," said he: "I ain't used to the road, but I'm bound to know what you're drivin' fur. Now, let's locate our discovery stake, 'n take our bearin's. You don't handle pick 'n sledge jest fur amusement, or yer shattered constitution. What do you figger on, — town-lots, or rich quartz, or what 'n thunder?"

"Patience!" said Joe.

Sam Wetherill swallowed the first word that came to his lips, and sat in silence for a while, trying to get up a substitute less objectionable, and equally expressive of his feeling. But the vocabulary of ejaculations is small at best, and the habit of profanity narrows it still further. Nobody is so hopelessly stuck for a word as the man who suddenly suppresses a convenient oath. So Mr. Wetherill, in despair, whistled softly to himself a bar of "My name it is Joe Bowers," and then, looking up, remarked, "Thar's a good prospect for that. Putty much every thing that happens 'll assay well enough, 'n yield rich in the pans too, ef all you want to git out of it is patience, and not bullion."

"Yes," said Joe: "all things work together."

"Well, I give it up," replied Sam. "All I got to say is, you do as I tell you, 'n git yerself a pardner. When you 'n him work together, as you say, I hope you'll strike something that pays better 'n patience — though I expect that pays too, in the long-run, when a fellow comes to the last big clean-up." And the honest miner, stepping down the zigzag trail to the cañon, disappeared in the gathering shadows.

Thanksgiving Joe continued for a month his quiet and regular life; then he took a partner after a fashion which rendered this natural and advisable step one of the most surprising of the many unusual features of his career in Silver Sheen. Everybody said he'd " be blowed," when he first heard of it; and about half the camp bet two to one with the other half that it wasn't true, the takers being secretly of that opinion themselves, but accepting the odds just to make things lively. A very positive skeptic (no people are so positive, by the way, as those who assume the negative) went so far, on being assured of the circumstance by Joe himself, as to offer to put up five dollars that Joe was mistaken. And Col. Gore, scarcely ever at a loss for words, was fairly staggered to express what at last he called the "preposterosity" of the story. For, according to the statements of the parties concerned, this meekest, mildest, quietest, and thankfullest of men had selected, out of a camp full of friends, the only man who was not his friend, — Bill Hazard, the new hand on the night-shift at the Desdemona: a fellow who was set down as a "rough," and quietly let alone. If anybody — even Joe — had killed him, it would have been reckoned nothing astonishing; and the presumption would have been strong, in the absence of evidence, that "Bill must 'a' drawed on the other feller first." But that any one not himself a "rough" should join hands with Bill for any honest purpose was amazing beyond explanation.

Yet Mr. William Hazard bore an appearance which strangely belied his reputation. He was handsome almost to effeminacy, with a smooth, pale-dark beauty which neither sun nor wind seemed to affect. But the delicacy of his face was striking at a distance only: upon a closer view it was perceived to bear the nameless shadow of evil passions, — a soft face grown hard. But some things distinguished Bill Hazard from his class. He did not drink, — that was not so strange: many of these men are practically teetotalers; but they usually abstain from stimulants because they are gamblers, and wish to be, under all circumstances, masters of themselves; whereas Hazard did not play cards, — and, strangest of all, he never indulged in that cheap vice, which, since it affects directly neither the personal efficiency of the individual, nor the property interests of the community, is apt to be universally allowed and practiced in rude settlements: I mean profanity, "the only thing," as Sam Wetherill once said (after he had given it up, by the way, "swore off"), — "the only thing that a real *poor* sinner could git cheap."

This freedom from all vices was one great element that helped to make Bill Hazard intolerable to his companions. Their instincts read clearly the principle which they could not have put in words, that true goodness of nature involves good nature. Perhaps Sam, after all, expressed it philosophically when he said, "These yer bad habits are the devil's contrivances, you bet; 'n he catches many a poor feller's soul that never meant no harm. But I've knowed fellers to strike it rich, 'n make a home stake, 'n just take their Wells Fargo drafts, 'n git for the East, 'n hunt up their old folks, or mebbe their wives 'n young uns, 'n leave off their liquor, 'n never touch a card — why, ef you'd ask 'em to 'ante up,' they wouldn't know what you meant; 'n all these yer devil's traps was clean busted for *them*. But when you clap your eyes on one of them smooth fellers like Bill Hazard, 's hard 'n 's barren's cap-rock, you don't want no further news about *him*. The devil's *in* him: he don't go for to waste no bad habits on a sure thing like that."

No, Sam was not quite correct. He overlooked a deeper-lying truth. The vices that brutalize men are dead weights that hang upon them for ever: no cure can enable him to walk in the full, erect stature of manhood who has bent earthward for years under such burdens. And, on the other hand, souls may be hardened by malign passion, which, nevertheless, being smitten aright, shall suddenly be transformed, and Lucifer become again the Son of the Morning. Hatred, akin to love, has somewhat of love's preserving power. It may ward off meaner fiends; and though its condor talons, and dark, brooding wings are surely fatal in the end to its helpless captive, yet, if frightened from its nest in time, it may soar gloomily away, to return no more, and leave behind the rescued soul like a child unharmed.

Thanksgiving Joe, replying to the remark of Sam Wetherill above quoted, put the argument in a homelier way:—

"I don't know about that, Sam: it is a good deal like sickness. When I had my fever, I should never have pulled through unless I had been helped by my good constitution. A man may have one thing pretty bad, and get over it; but, if he has too many things ailing him at once, it's a poor show for the doctors. Now, if Will was only cured of the one thing that troubles him, I think he would be a pretty healthy man; whereas you boys, if you don't look out, will get yourselves tangled up with so many diseases, that your moral constitutions will be just disintegrated, like any old outcrop, and nothing will take hold of you. And thank God!" added Joe softly, half to himself, "I believe I can cure him."

Sam was surprised to hear the new partner called "Will,"— a form of his name which no one else in the camp employed. It argued even affection for him; being as far removed from the ceremonious "Mr.," on one hand, as from the "Bill" of mere ordinary acquaintanceship, on the other. But he made no comment, and presently sauntered homeward, more than ever convinced that Thanksgiving Joe was "too good for this yer style o' thing," and would certainly get into trouble with his kind heart and foggy head, if some friend without too tender a conscience did not stand between him and the perilous results of his unsuspicious kindness. The conclusion of this train of thought was a resolve to "keep an eye on that Hazard; 'n if he tried any games on Joe, jest put a hole in him."

This was the evening of the day on which the partnership had been formed. It had been negotiated at sunrise, as the day-shift going into the Desdemona met the night-shift coming out. Bill Hazard, coming out of the mine, looked up, as if drawn by a strange, horrid fascination, to the long white outcrop of the Mammoth vein, that caught the first tints of day, and stood out clearly over the dimness of the deep cañon. Then he turned away with set teeth, as if the sight both pained and angered him, and, as he turned, felt on his shoulder the hand of Thanksgiving Joe, whose face was moved as if with the emotion of a sudden recognition. Hazard glanced at him carelessly, and started to pass on. But Joe detained him, and said simply, —

"I want a partner, and I must have you. There's my place, yonder, on the hill. Come up to-night, and talk it over."

Something in the tone of Joe's voice startled the listener. It was like a voice, perhaps, that he had heard before; but as he hurriedly glanced again at the speaker, who had partly turned from him to point out the cabin on the mountain, he saw only the white hair and beard and the stooping shoulders. It was certainly a stranger. Yet he could not command a perfect cynical indifference in replying to the stranger's words. There was a shade of sadness in his answer, —

"If you talk it over, you'll change your mind. You made some mistake in your man."

"Then I won't talk it over," replied Joe. "Call it settled. No mistake, thank God! — on *my* part. I shall expect you. You know where to find me." And, with another gesture toward his cabin, he moved away.

"No, not there," ejaculated Bill Hazard fiercely. The other was already some distance away; and his features were not distinctly seen as he paused at these words, and stood with his back to the morning; but his voice carried mingled compassion and command.

"Yes, there!" said he, and, swiftly striding towards the mine, met the rest of the night-shift hasting homeward. At the same moment he overtook his own companions: the two parties were mingled.

"My last day with you, boys," he remarked cheerfully. "Will Hazard and I are going to try our luck as partners."

Thus the surprising news was conveyed in a trice to the two classes that composed the population of Silver Sheen, — namely, those who worked by day, and those who worked by night. Before Joe came out of the Desdemona at the close of his shift, in the afternoon, everybody had heard of it.

After Sam Wetherill's brief call that evening at the cabin, Thanksgiving Joe sat alone, waiting for the other visitor whom he expected. His usual calm demeanor seemed to have forsaken him. He piled brush on the smoldering fire where he had cooked his supper, until it flamed like the beacon that Hero set to guide the course of her coming lover. By its blazing light he strove to see down the path that led to the cañon, but to his dazzled eyes the shadows were darker than before. Far below, like stars reflected, twinkled the candles in many a window; but between them and him was a black gulf. Drawing from his pocket a worn newspaper, he began to read, by way of enforcing patience; but nothing attracted his interest until his eye fell upon a bold head-line introducing the governor's proclamation of Thanksgiving Day. The name reminded him of his own *sobriquet*, and he glanced down the lines as if the announcement had some special meaning for him. The governor, not unwilling to combine business with worship, had painted in brilliant colors the productiveness of the mines of the State, and hinted, as additional cause for gratitude, that new discoveries well worthy of the attention of capitalists were daily made. That part Joe passed over with a smile, thinking, perhaps, of his Mammoth vein, and its perfidious "base metal." Over another paragraph he paused with brightening looks. It alluded to the circumstance that all the States now observed, in accordance with the President's recommendation, a simultaneous Thanksgiving Day. His thoughts wandered far to the East, over deserts and mountains, and the great plains and the great rivers, to the Jersey village which he had not seen for five years; from which, since his fever, two years ago, he had not heard. The memory was disquieting; for it was his own course alone that had thus cut him off — from whom? Only one friend; and she only a friend. It was Thanksgiving Day, too, when he saw her last. The parson's sermon — he had forgotten it, all but the text: that Jenny had written out for him, to satisfy a whim of his; and he had folded up the paper, and carried it night and day ever since. If he had spoken plainly that night, would she have become more than a friend? Alas, perhaps! — yet no, no.

A hundred times he had been thankful that she was ignorant of his love and his sacrifice; that he had left her with a pleasant farewell, expecting to return, after two or three years, with money enough to justify him in asking for her hand; that he had never betrayed his feelings in those friendly letters which he had sent so regularly, and which were so regularly answered until — ah! he must not think of that. Her dear letters were all destroyed. He had burned them himself, keeping only the Thanksgiving text, and vowing, for her sake, and his own soul's sake, and the sake — of him whom Jenny loved, to live apart from her, save in his secret thoughts, and, haply, in the life to come. To-morrow was Thanksgiving Day again, and he tried to think it a good omen. His sacrifice was not complete: to-night, he hoped, would happily perfect his work. Yet the pain of loss was not wholly dead; and even at this moment he would give worlds to undo utterly, so that it could be as if it had not been, the scheme which he was nevertheless ready to give his life, if need be, to consummate. For a man is still a man; and Joe was only thirty, for all his white hairs.

Absorbed in thought, he heeded not the sound of climbing feet, until a step close at hand aroused him. As he sprang up and stood erect, with the fire-light full upon him, William Hazard strode suddenly out of the darkness, looked for an instant with an intense, bewildered, frightened gaze, into his eyes, and staggered speechless back against the corner of the cabin, staring as at a ghost. The governor's proclamation fell from Joe's hands, which were stretched out in hearty welcome.

"Don't look at me that way, Will," he said. "I see you know me now, though you did not this morning. I'm changed since my fever, — but not in my heart toward you."

The stony look of fright passed from the pale, young face, the hard lines softened; but Will Hazard still shrank from the clasp of Joe's welcoming hands. "Shoot," he said, folding his arms across his breast: "it's your turn, and I'm glad of it!"

"Amen!" replied the deep voice of Thanksgiving Joe. "It *is* my turn: your life belongs to me. Is it not so?"

His visitor nodded without speaking, and gloomily smiled his contempt for the worthless existence alluded to.

"I suppose I may spare it, if I prefer that way," said Joe.

"As you choose," replied Hazard.

"As I was saying this morning," continued Joe, with a quiet consciousness of the power over a desperate soul which this strange interview had for a moment given him, "I want a partner, and you are the man. I told you to come here and talk it over; and you have come. Now, if I kill you, how can we talk it over?" he added slowly, and rubbed his hands together in mute applause at the triumphant argument. "There's some mistake, Will. You gave me no chance to explain, otherwise you could not have thought I was your enemy." Then, suddenly changing his manner, he asked, "Have you heard from Jenny Lockhart?"

"What is the use of tormenting me with her name?" returned Will. "She is the cause of all the trouble. A woman is not worth a friend; and for that woman I threw my friend away. I loved you, George, till the devil of jealousy took possession of me. When I left the States, three years ago, she had promised to be my wife. You were her cousin and my friend. She wrote to you, and you read me her letters. They were pleasant, cousinly letters, and I liked to hear them. I did not tell you of the love-letters she wrote at the same time to me. I wanted to watch you. I suspected you of receiving others of which you said nothing.

"You carried in your belt a paper which you never showed. I felt sure it contained your secret. I tried to get it without your knowledge; but you kept it always on your body, night and day. At last you did receive a letter — a letter from her — which you did not show to me. I saw you read it, at night, by the light of the camp-fire, when you thought I was asleep. You put your head in your hands, and sat a long time. Then you took from your bosom a package of letters, put them all in the fire with the one you had just read, and watched them till they were burned up. You took that paper from your belt, as if you would burn that too; and, as you did so, I prepared to spring out of my blanket, and seize it. I was determined to know what was in it. But you read it through, shook your head, and put it back in your belt.

"The next day as we were exploring, two or three miles from our camp, we came over the summit to the head of this cañon. You know well enough what happened. You sat down close by this spot, on the croppings of that ledge, and began to tell me that you had received a letter from Jenny. It was too much for me to bear: I had been cursing over it all night, anyhow. I hated her and you as a pair of double-dealing deceivers. I forgot that she only was deceiving me: *you* could not know that I was engaged to her. I interrupted you fiercely, charged you with treachery, demanded the secret paper from you, and, without waiting for your answer, sprang upon you in a fury to snatch the belt from your waist.

"We fell together. I swear to you, George Graham, that I did not draw my revolver. It went off by accident. But the rage of murder was in my heart; and it seemed to me as if my black thoughts had become hands, and fired the pistol. You fainted, I suppose. I thought I had killed you, and I fled like Cain. But I would have come back to you, only I saw from a distance a party approaching. They came, as if guided by a pointing hand, straight to the spot where you lay. I saw them take you up, and knew by their angry gestures, and their keen looks in every direction, that they were determined to hunt down your murderer. At first I would have returned, and surrendered myself; but, when some of them started in the direction where I crouched, the instinct of fear took hold on me, and I ran. They neither caught nor discovered me; and I found my way to Austin, to Virginia City, to Unionville, to Boise, to Helena, to Salt Lake, to Denver, to Santa Fé, to Prescott and Tucson, to La Paz, and San Diego, to San Francisco, Sacramento, Yreka,— everywhere, with the devil in my heart.

"Two desires tortured me for ever. I could not destroy them, and I dared not fulfill them. One was to return to this place, gain some news of you, and find at least your grave. The other was to go back to Jersey, meet Jenny Lockhart, tell her of the ruin she had brought on honest men,— how one had lost his life, and the other his soul, by her faithlessness, and so make her taste a share of the bitterness that I felt. I couldn't do it — I — in short, I loved the girl yet, in spite of all she had done, and I despised myself for it. I'm bad enough,— too bad, in fact, to take any pleasure in the beastly sins of these low-lived wretches. I don't like mankind well enough to drink or gamble with them. I don't fight them even, though they seem to think me a desperate fellow, who would as soon kill a dozen of them as not. Bah! if a man simply despises them, they think he must want their blood. Sots, thieves, and murderers: that's their classification of society. They were right, so far as I am concerned. I was a murderer in passion, and I thought in deed; but the business had no such attractions as to make me intend to carry it on wholesale and for life.

"I'll not make a long story of it. But you wanted to talk it over, and you had better hear me out. When I am done, I am done. I don't play the repentant sinner with you, George Graham. It seems to me there is no room and no use for repentance. I could love you — if you could trust me again; but that's impossible. Your forgiveness I don't want. What I want is to pay my debt. I will not be your partner; but, if you will let me work for you, it will be a better reparation than I expected to make when I came up here to-night. I came here, as I came to this camp a fortnight ago, because I couldn't keep away. When they talked of Thanksgiving Joe, and showed me your cabin, on the very spot that was the most dreadful to me in all the world, I knew in my soul that somehow my fate was fastened to yours. I thought you had my secret, and would be my judge. I wouldn't let anybody tell me the story of Thanksgiving Joe — the name was awful to me. And at last you found me, and called me — and I came to my doom. It is better than I dreamed. Even I can give thanks to know that George Graham, hated and wronged, was not killed outright by the hand of his treacherous friend.

"George, I will do for you what man may do. Perhaps you may some day begin to trust me over again, and lay the blame of my crime upon the woman who betrayed us both."

During this long speech neither of the parties had moved. Will Hazard stood, at its conclusion, with his arms still folded, and looked into the fire. He had kept his eyes fixed on the glowing brands, speaking in low, measured tones, as if another spoke through him. But George Graham had never removed his keen gaze from the face of his friend; and now he stepped forward once more, laid his hand upon Will's shoulder, and said, —

"Thank God, you love her yet!"

The young man, taken by surprise at this sudden assault, started, and tried to speak. But George went on, with simple, quaint gravity, —

"No: it is my turn now. Come here and sit down. As I said before, I want a partner. Now we're going to talk it over. You're all wrong, Will. If you had seen the letter I burned, you would know that Jenny Lockhart was true as steel to you. She told me in that letter — what you had not let me know. She begged me to be your friend always, as I had been hers. I — I'd rather not talk about that night. It's all past now, you know," said George, with a tremor of his voice. Will did not perceive it: he was too much absorbed in the effect of the discovery upon his own feelings.

"Then you didn't love her, after all!" he cried: "you were only her cousin and friend!"

There was a moment's silence ; and then George answered, like an echo from afar, "Yes, her cousin and friend."

"But you burned up her letters?" pursued the young man, so eagerly following the clew of the riddle that seemed to hold his happiness as to forget entirely for the moment his recent attitude of confessed culprit. "And you kept one?"

Thanksgiving Joe, with slow and steady hand, unbuckled his belt, took from it the folded paper, opened it, and handed it to him, saying, without further explanation, "We'll burn that too."

Will read, bewildered, the words which seemed so far from being the shrine of any special secret. "'Let us come before his presence with Thanksgiving.' There is nothing in that!"

Thanksgiving Joe silently stretched out his hand, took back the paper, replaced it in his belt, and, with a simplicity that was more baffling than diplomacy, resumed the thread of his discourse. "As I was saying, I want a partner. To-morrow morning you'll write to Jenny; and we two will go to work in earnest. It won't be long before you can go back to her. We are wiser than we were. It isn't worth while to spend a lifetime trying to get ready to begin. Jenny don't want you to be rich. She said so in — in that letter. When we get a good mine, you can go home, and leave me to work it. I am better off out here: I've got used to the country. I mean to live and die out here somewhere. And if you and Jenny will write to me — why, I won't burn your letters any more."

This pleasantry had a mournful tone that would have revealed to any disinterested observer the sorrow that lurked beneath. But Will's thoughts were miles away; and, when he recalled them, it was only for self-reproach. He lamented gloomily his unworthiness, and declared, that, though heaven now opened before him, he dared not set his foot upon the threshold. "No, George," he said, "I owe the rest of my life to you. If we could go back together — but what folly! Here we sit, as poor as your old Mammoth vein there, and dream of happiness. I have earned and squandered money enough in these two years past to make our dreams come true; but now I must reap what I have sown. It was almost better to believe her false."

He rose gloomily as he spoke, and George did not detain him. His morbid mind could not be all at once restored to health. It was better to let him be alone for a while, and realize his new position. So George rose also, and the two men clasped hands for a brief farewell. An instant they stood thus, and then, by a common impulse, kissed each other. It was the pledge of reconciliation and hope. The terms of their relation seemed to be settled by it; for they parted with an air of familiarity, and with no more formal words than, "Well, good-night, old fellow. Take care of yourself. See you in the morning." Whereat Thanksgiving Joe went straightway into his cabin, and Will Hazard took the path down the cañon. The former, exhausted by the interview, but at peace with himself, rolled into his bunk, and soon slept soundly; but the latter stopped half way down the hill, seated himself on a rock, and gave himself up to wakeful meditation.

All this time the governor's proclamation of Thanksgiving had lain unnoticed where it had fallen from Joe's hands. The fire had burned nearly out; but a few coals remained, to brighten occasionally as a puff of the night-wind touched them. At every puff, moreover, the newspaper with the governor's proclamation hitched a little nearer to the fire. Between times it paused, or seemed to retreat; then, by rolling over, and sliding swiftly forward, it made up every loss of ground. It seemed to be alive, and hesitating, while it advanced, to carry out some plan of mischief. At last, with a leap of undisguised intent, it fell upon the embers, swept across them, bursting into flame as it did so, and, flying over the short intervening space, clung like a fiery monster to the dry, resinous piñon-stems of the cabin, within which, unconscious of his peril, lay Thanksgiving Joe.

A moment later Will Hazard was aware of a lurid light that threw his own shadow in front of him, and, starting from his revery, turned to see wrapped in flames the cabin he had recently left. His trumpet-call of "Fire!" brought the miners from their work or sleep; and a dozen men were soon hastening up the hillside. But Will had the start of them by a long ascent; and with flying feet he sped to the cabin, shouting as he bounded up the rocky steep.

Thanksgiving Joe was dreaming of a quiet Jersey village-church, and a sweet face therein, when he was aroused by the shouts, and sprang up bewildered to find himself surrounded with smoke and flame. A step through the scorching circle would have placed him in safety; but alas! in his confusion he rushed in the wrong direction, and, instead of escaping by the door in front, stumbled over the pile of rock and ore at the rear of his cabin, and fell headlong into the shaft of the Mammoth. A second after, Will Hazard leaped through the blazing ruins, calling his friend's name. The bed, the room, were empty; but a feeble voice replied from the depths to his frantic call, and by the light of the burning cabin he saw Thanksgiving Joe lying helpless, twelve feet below him, at the bottom of the shaft.

The first miners that arrived met Will carrying in his arms a heavy burden, the body of his friend.

Thanksgiving Joe (by this name he was best known to them and to us) had fainted away. Tenderly they carried him to the nearest cabin, and applied their simple means of restoration. But for hours they could not bring him back to consciousness.

It was during this period that Sam Wetherill, who had been foremost in service by the bunk of the sufferer, stepped to where Will Hazard sat in a stupor of grief, touched him on the shoulder, and beckoned him to follow. He was obeyed, and presently the two men stood together in the open air. The dawn was breaking.

"Look here!" said Sam quietly. "This yer business has got to be explored. I was at Joe's cabin last night, and I know he was expectin' you. If you've got any remarks to make, you might as well make 'em to me — unless you prefer a committee."

This allusion to lynch law did not move the nerves of the pale young man, whose reputation as a desperado seemed now likely to put him in peril.

"If George Graham dies," said he, "I shall not want to live."

Sam turned, with a quick revulsion of feeling.

"You knowed him? you loved him?" said he. "He was the best man in the sage-brush. Thar warn't no discount on him. He warn't no slouch. He was a man — Give us your hand!" And the discovery of a big burn, hitherto unheeded, on Will Hazard's hand, furnished final testimony to his sincere efforts for the rescue of Thanksgiving Joe.

At this moment occurred another incident, for the preliminary explanation of which a few words are required.

Redhead Pete, it will be remembered, has gone on one of his periodical hunts after the Lost Silver Mine. For many days, nothing has been heard from him. But now, in the cold, first light of the morning, he comes over the summit, ragged, hirsute, defeated, but not conquered. Once more his quest has failed, yet the hope which inspired it springs eternal in his heart.

He pauses at the sight of the smoldering ruins of Joe's cabin. No one is near to explain the mystery. Pete walks to the edge of the shaft, among the smoking brands, and reflectively turns over with his booted foot the blackened fragments of Joe's pile of worthless ore. "This yer base metal," he mutters — but suddenly he stoops, seizes a stone, rubs it up and down on his buckskin breeches to clean its surface, and eagerly examines a dozen little whitish pellets that seem to be clinging to it like drops of perspiration. As a final test, he takes out his jack-knife, and cuts into one of them. It is pure silver!

Pete is no fool. His credulity towards Shoshones and their legends does not prevent him now from behaving like a wise and prudent man. He walks to the end of Joe's claim on the Mammoth, and there erects one of the half-burnt poles of the cabin, on which he rudely carves the words, " Ex. No. 1, South,

Peter Jackson." Then, and not before, he comes down into the quiet, solemn camp, leaping from rock to rock, with hair and arms flying abroad, and whooping and shouting: —

"Whar's Thanksgiving Joe? Whar is he? That thar ledge o' his'n 's the clear bullion: the ore only wants to be burnt, 'n the silver jest biles out of it."

And so, bestowing on the air and on the distant ears of men his reckless and fragmentary explanations, he rushes downward to the spot where Sam and Will are standing. Their sad faces hush him at once. But Thanksgiving Joe, lying until now unconscious within the cabin, has been roused by the shouts, has recognized his name, has opened his eyes, and looked around upon the sorrowful company, as for some missing face. Divining his mute request, the colonel steps to the door, and calls in the three who stand outside. As they enter, Joe looks inquiringly upon them. Sam takes his hand.

"All right, old man!" says Sam. "You jest shake yerself, 'n you'll git over this. Thar's good news at last. That thar Mammoth Ledge, as we all thought was base metal, was jest nothin' but this yer roastin' ore, like what they tell of up to Austin, — base metal ef you try to work it wet, 'n putty nigh the clear spoon metal if you jest warm it up with fire aforehand."

Candor compels me to state that several of the sympathetic audience glide quietly from the room during these brief remarks, and, on getting outside the house, begin a fierce race to the Mammoth claim, — a proceeding which Redhead Pete, secure in the possession of Extension No. 1, South, regards with quiet amusement.

Thanksgiving Joe listens intelligently. "Thank God!" his faint voice murmurs, breaking into the familiar ascription for the last time. Then, gathering his strength, he says with an effort, but distinctly, —

"Gentlemen, my name is George Graham. This man, William Hazard, is my dear friend and partner. He is half-owner in the Mammoth claim; and the half-interest that belongs to me — I hereby — give and bequeath — to him — in trust — for Miss Janet Lockhart — he knows. Sam, you will see the papers straight?"

Sam nods. "Whatever you say, Joe, is better'n law in *this* camp. There's nobody here that'll go back on your words."

A murmur of subdued assent runs round the room. Will Hazard falls on his knees by the bunk, and buries his face in the blanket. Thanksgiving Joe, still holding Sam Wetherill's hand in one of his own, lays the other upon Will's clustering hair.

"Give her my love, Will," he says, and closes his eyes for several minutes. The stillness is broken only by sobs from the kneeling figure of Hazard. At last the dying man looks up once more.

"My belt," he says. They had taken it off when they were hunting upon his body for the injuries, which, being, alas! internal, could neither be found nor cured. Now they bring it to him, and once more his fingers feebly seek the precious paper which it contains. He draws it forth, reads with fading sight the well-known lines. A wave of peace glides over his face, an expression of unutterable gratitude. Soundlessly his lips form the solemn "Amen." The hand falls lifeless — Joe has obeyed the summons of the Almighty Father, and entered into his presence with thanksgiving.

AGAMEMNON:

A STORY OF CALIFORNIA.

I.

YOUNG BULLION.

"HOT? You bet it's hot! A cool one hundred and fifteen in the shade!" So Stephen Moore, the stage-driver, paradoxically described the weather, while he watered his horses from a rather slimy-looking spring by a solitary cabin among the foot-hills. Before him were barren reaches of dusty white ascending road, their ridges dotted with black spots of scrub-oak, then beyond all the blue line of the High Sierra. Behind him the great plain of California, or rather that portion of it which lies around and south of Tulare Lake, shimmered in the heat, and sent up little dust whirlwinds that traveled hither and thither over its glowing surface like slender pillars of cloud. In a few years the desert would blossom, and miles upon miles of golden harvest would wave where now the wild oats and grasses, early browned by sultry summer, only mimicked the husbandry of man. A little later the locomotive would shoot and toot through these spacious solitudes. But that time was not yet; and as it is said to be darkest just before daybreak, so it seemed most lonely in the land just before it was going to become most "lively."

"Yes, *sir*," said Stephen, "one hundred and fifteen, if it's an inch! But you don't feel the heat here as you do in the States. Why, ninety on Broadway just knocks the people over right and left with sunstrokes. But there's Young Bullion there, a-sleeping on the coach, with his hat off, and his face to the sun, and not taking any harm, either."

Stephen's remarks were addressed to the passenger who shared with him the driver's seat, — a young man of whose personal appearance at that moment little can be said, since, like everybody else who had traveled that day along the valley road, with the wind dead in the rear, he was so covered with dust as to be all of one color from head to foot, except where his eyes peeped out under their dusty lashes, like clean children at the window of an adobe cabin. It is not necessary to say much concerning this young man. He has little to do with the story, except to tell it; for the truth must out. It was the present narrator who sat as aforesaid on the day above mentioned, while Stephen watered the horses, and Young Bullion slept sprawling on the top of the coach. Having confessed so much, it is hardly worth while to keep the traveler who tells this story in the chilly and unconfidential position of a third person any longer; and he will therefore, with the reader's permission, speak of himself, as folks usually do, in the first person.

I was going up into the mountains to visit a newly-discovered mining-district when Stephen first called my attention to Young Bullion, as narrated above. I had not noticed him before; but this was easily explained by the fact that I had only just got a chance to ride outside, the seat having been occupied from Stockton by an exasperating old cattle-breeder, who never wanted to change places with an inside passenger. Heat, dust, night, sleep, wind, — whatever usually disposes the outsider to make such a temporary exchange, — had no effect upon him. But at last we came to a ranche where the cattle-breeder alighted for good, leaving my friend Stephen free to offer the seat by his side to me, whom he called "Professor," because I was going up to inspect mines. In the Middle West it is "Judge" or "Kernel:" in the Far West "Professor" has been added to the list of handy titles for strangers.

Stephen and I were not strangers, however. We had made many a trip together on the Wells-Fargo coaches in California, Oregon, and Nevada; and once we had started for a real vacation-spree, gone through the Yosemite, the Hetch-Hetchy, up to the headwaters of the Tuolumne, and so on through the High Sierra, away to the mighty cañons of Kern and King Rivers, camping on the bare ground at night, wherever we could find water and grass for our horses. So we had plenty to talk about now that we had met again; and, when I climbed to my place by his side, I paid no attention to the form that lay stretched on the still higher seat, behind the driver's.

But at the next stopping-place, as I have already remarked, Stephen mentioned the sleeping passenger as "Young Bullion;" and this caused me to turn and inspect him. He was so short, that he lay at full-length upon the seat, without hanging over his feet, or doubling up his legs, as experience had taught me I must needs do when I tried to sleep in that situation. The freckled face, light yellow hair, and brown stubby hand, presented nothing extraordinary. It was evidently a mere boy, exposing his complexion in a way which his mother would have disapproved, had she known he was so emphatically "out."

"What makes you call him 'Young Bullion'?" I asked, surveying his coarse, patched clothes, and failing to see any special indications of the precious metal about him.

"Well," replied Stephen, as he swashed the horses' legs with the water they had left in the pail, "it's a name the boys gave him, over at Pactolus district. He discovered the district; and he owns the best claim on the best mine there, — the biggest thing on the coast, they say, next to the Comstock."

As this was a statement which I had heard concerning a score of mines at different times, I was not as deeply thrilled by it as a tyro might have been; and it was with some indifference that I said, "Ah! what's the name of the mine?"

"The Agamemnon," said Stephen. "It's named after him. Agamemnon's his real name."

That did give me a little start; for the Agamemnon mine in Pactolus district was the very property I had been sent from San Francisco to examine. But I reflected that many claims might be located side by side on the same lode, and doubtless some other part than that which belonged to this boy had attracted the notice of my clients. At all events, I preserved a due professional reticence as to my own business, and remarked only, "Agamemnon is a queer name. Agamemnon what?"

By this time the driver was mounting again; and, before he could answer my question, he had to unwind the reins from the break-bar, arrange them properly in the gloved fingers of his left hand, pick up his long-lashed whip from the top of the coach, then take off the break, and tell the horses pithily to "Git!" These operations were scarcely completed, when Young Bullion suddenly sat upright, and replied in person to my inquiry, which he must have overheard.

"Agamemnon Atrides O'Ballyhan," said he, with a

twinkle in his shrewd gray eyes. "The boys call it Bullion when the old man ain't around. 'Twouldn't suit the old man, you bet!"

"Who is the old man?—your father?" I said.

"Oh, no!" he replied gravely. "My son."

Seeing my look of blank amazement, Stephen interposed the explanation that this was the jocose way in which the camp chose to consider the relationship.

"Well," said Agamemnon, "how's a feller to know, except by what folks say? And think I'd let the old man play father around my place? He couldn't run the machine a day."

"I was somewhat displeased by this disrespectful tone; but I let it pass without comment, partly because the atmosphere was not favorable to lectures on filial piety, and partly because I was following in my mind a suggested coincidence. To make myself certain, I took out my note-book, and sought the address of the party to whom I was to apply for permission to inspect the Agamemnon mine. It was, as I had supposed, Mr. O'Ballyhan. Turning to the boy, who had watched my movements keenly, I said, "I think it must be your father with whom I have some business."

"Who? The old man? Business? Not much! If you've got any business, it's with *me:* you just rest easy on that! Come up from the Bay to look at the Agamemnon ledge, now, hain't you? Well, I'm your man! Oh! you needn't go for to doubt my word.

I'm the only fust-class, responsible, business O'Ballyhan on the Pacific coast. Bet ye what ye like. Put up yer money, 'n leave it to Steve. No, I won't! Don't bet; swore off. Never did, very heavy, anyhow. But Steve there, he'll tell yer it's all right. Go in, Steve! If he won't believe yer, bet with him yerself, 'n leave it to the first bullwhacker ye meet."

But I was ready to accept Steve's assurance that this premature young adventurer was actually the mine-owner with whom my clients were negotiating. A very little further conversation soon put this point beyond the shadow of a doubt.

"You've been pretty lively," said he. "Thought I'd be one coach ahead o' ye, and git a chance to open up the mine a little. But I had to stop over at Stockton to buy some powder and steel. Got a new kind o' powder,— this yer giant powder: made the feller show me how to use it. We went out o' town half a mile, an' couldn't find no rocks: so we blowed a scrub-oak all to sawdust. That's how I lost a day."

"Have you been in San Francisco?" I inquired. "It is strange that my friends did not mention it."

"Think I'd let 'em know I was there?" he replied with a wink. "I'll tell ye jest what I did: went down to Stockton with twelve mules an' a big load o' fust-class Agamemnon ore,— this yer black sulphuret, free gold sprinkled all through it, an' put it in the fire, an' the silver sweats out to boot,— sent it down from Stockton by boat, an' sot on the bags myself, you bet, all the way, with a six-shooter in my pocket. Soon's I'd got it down thar all safe, 'n locked up in a warehouse, I went off to git some dinner. When the waiter fetched the pork 'n beans, I kind o' liked his looks; 'n says I, 'I want a agent for a little bit o' business here in town, 'n I guess you're my man.' He laughed at fust; thought I was fool'n' him, or else was a fool myself. But I fixed that quick enough. Says I, 'Now don't go for to think you can take me in because I'm small. Ye can't come no tricks over me. I've got fifteen tons o' fust-class Agamemnon ore to sell, all picked and sacked. Here's a fair sample, 'n there's plenty more whar that came from. If you want to sell it for me, 'n earn a hundred dollars easy, say so.'

"Well, his eyes stuck out so when he see my sample, that he looked half scared to death. But he was glad enough to be my agent. He was a big swell when he was dressed up, 'n he could make a powerful impression, only not on me. 'I ain't what I was,' says he, while we was a-talkin': 'I've seen better days.'—'Now you jest come down,' says I: 'I don't want no more o' *that!* Git enough f'm m' old man. As for you, ye're putty nigh what ye always was 'n always will be, 'n y' hain't seen no better day 'n this one'll be, if ye behave yerself.'

"'Young man,' says he, 'you ought to be respeckful to yer elders.'

"'Elders!' says I, hollerin' like mad,—'who d'ye

call elders? I was born in the year one, 'n I'm eighteen hundred 'n sixty-five years old, A.D., U.S.: d'ye hear that?' Then I laid my six-shooter alongside o' my plate; 'n says I, 'I'll be obliged to you if you'll call me Mr. O'Ballyhan.'

"Well, that's the way I got my agent. He was the politest feller, after that, you ever see. When he went round to a big house in Market Street, where they was a-buyin' ores to send to Europe, me 'n my six-shooter just went along. 'No shenannigan, James,' says I. 'We'll just wait on the doorstep, 'n protect ye when ye come out.' Well, after a few minutes he comes out, 'n says, 'If the rest o' the lot is like the sample, they'll give a thousand dollars a ton for it.' — 'Not much,' says I: 'they'll have it assayed, and they'll make a bid accordin', that's what they'll do.' An' that's what they did do, 'n gimme twenty thousand dollars for that lot of ore, rather 'n lemme go. Wouldn't 'a' sold it for that, either, only they began to talk about the mine, 'n said they'd probably like to buy her. When my agent told me that, I says, 'Well, I hain't no partic'lar objection. She's a good mine, 'n I wouldn't retire from her for less 'n a hundred thousand dollars. If they wan't her at that price, they can take her — or they can leave her. An' if you sell her, James,' says I, 'you'll get a thousand on top o' your hundred.' Well, there was big talk an' lots of it for a couple o' days; but I kept quiet 'n out o' sight, 'n James he negotiated till you couldn't rest. Fust thing they wanted was a report. Sent 'em one that the old man wrote and printed in 'The Pactolus Weekly Nozzle.' The old man is hefty on a report: he jist slings the ink, now, I tell ye! About all he kin do."

I remarked that I had seen the report. It was indeed an extraordinary sample, even of that extraordinary kind of literature. It abounded in gorgeous descriptions of the beauty of the natural scenery, the immense display of geological phenomena, the unlimited amount of "yet undiscovered" treasure slumbering beneath the rocky surface, the salubrious climate, the exactly central geographical position (proved by drawing a circle round it on any map), and the metropolitan future, of Pactolus district. I remembered particularly the glowing conclusion: "The Gulch, to the golden sands of which this marvelous region owes its name, has long ceased to yield a suitable auriferous return to the honest hand of labor. [Note by the editor of "The Weekly Nozzle:" "But it will pay big to hydraulic."] But in the gold and silver veins which lie along certain magnetic lines in the rocks there are treasures surpassing those of the Lydian River, and which will be, in the words of the great Thucydides, *Ktema es aei*, — a thing forever."

Agamemnon continued, "They said that report wa'n't enough: so I sent word to 'em to send up their own man; 'n I expect you're the feller."

I replied that I was the feller.

"Thought so the minute I laid eyes on yer. Well, now, we'll jest hev a few plain words about this business, 'n perhaps they'll save you the trouble o' goin' any farther. S'pose yer know I've got to pay yer fee. Left the money in bank down 't the Bay."

I nodded assent.

"S'pose y' expect I'll give something **extry** if you make a good report, 'n the mine gets sold — hey?"

"Well," I said gravely, "it would be reasonable, wouldn't it?"

"Reasonable?" said he, with a steady light in his gray eyes, as he turned, and looked me full in the face. "I don't know about that. But it's jest impossible — d'ye hear that? You can go back to Frisco, unless yer want to examine somebody else's mine: yer can't git into the Agamemnon. There's goin' to be fair play with her, or nothin'." And with that he turned his back to me.

After an embarrassing silence, I said, "But, Mr. O'Ballyhan, you made the offer, didn't you?"

"Wanted to find ye out, 'n I found ye out," he replied curtly, without deigning to look at me.

"Well," I rejoined, "I wanted to find *you* out, and I've found *you* out. I'm very glad you regard it as dishonorable to give a bribe. If you had really tendered me one, I should have reported it to my clients, and advised them to drop the business."

"Too thin!" was Agamemnon's sole reply; and I saw on Steve's face a grin of intense amusement at my discomfiture.

"Look here!" said I as a last resort, "I'll leave it to Steve. He knows me; and he'll tell you that I am an honest man."

Steve could hardly resist the temptation to make matters worse by a dubious answer; but, seeing in my face that the trouble might be serious, he changed his tone, and gave to his remarks a satisfactory end.

"Well," he said slowly, "I don't know: it's my impression that he stole my last pipeful of Lone Jack, and smoked it himself in camp on the Tuolumne; and a man that would do that — hey, boys? No: he's all right, Young Bullion: he'll do the square thing by you. I know him."

Young Bullion turned, and held out his hand. "Put it there!" he said. And I "put it there," shaking hands with him in token of good faith. "Yer see," he continued presently, "th' ole man'll try it on. He's a disgrace to the family, he is. Don't you take nothin' — I mean no promises (he hain't got nothin' else to give you) — from th' ole man. I'm tryin' to reform him, I am: swore off lots o' things on his account ('n for some other partic'lar reasons). But soon's any stranger comes around, th' ole man slumps back agin into th' ole ways, — goes to gamblin' an' drinkin'. Ever play poker?"

I said I had no knowledge of that accomplishment.

"Well, I can play it with any man in Pactolus, or anywhere else. Th' ole man taught me himself. But I swore off f'm gamblin,' 'n I got all the boys to say they won't play with th' ole man: so he had to shut up. They wa'n't very sorry to promise: he used to clean 'em out every time. But it wasn't the square thing; 'n I — I — the name o' the O'Ballyhans is goin' to be kept clean after this, by — !" Was I mistaken, or did I see this premature young person dash a tear from his eye? Instantly I heard him mutter, " Thar, now, I've swore off swearin', 'n jist been 'n almost done it again!"

I need hardly say that by this time I was much interested in the strange character here presented for study. With mingled curiosity and respect I set myself to win his confidence, and extract an outline of his history. In spite of all his preternatural shrewdness and coolness, I found that he was at heart a boy, and required only the touch of sympathy and appreciation to make him talk freely. For more than an hour he ran on, with a queer mixture of simplicity and acuteness, narrating the experiences of an uneventful and yet heroic life; while Stephen and I listened without comment, except that the stage-driver nodded occasionally in confirmation of some statements that came within his own knowledge, or touched up his leaders with crackling emphasis when his feelings were particularly aroused.

II.

FURTHER ACQUAINTANCE.

I LEARNED that Agamemnon Atrides O'Ballyhan owed his classical name to the fancy of his father, — a graduate of Trinity College, Dublin, and a careless, jolly spendthrift, who, after running through his own inheritance and a small fortune brought him by his wife, had taken sudden leave of his creditors, and come to California in the early days, after the discovery of gold. His scraps of classical and mathematical learning found no market here. He had no solid attainments, no capacity for work, and no conscience: so, without much resistance, he yielded to the downward current, and became a gambler, perhaps worse. He was not fit to be an honest gambler, if I may use the paradox; that is to say, he could not rely upon skill and coolness to guarantee him a living in that profession, without resort to cheating, for he speedily became a drunkard also; and no successful gambler can afford to indulge that vice. The result was inevitable, — a vagabond life, interspersed with scenes of exposure and disgrace. From one mining-camp to another he dragged his wife and the young Agamemnon, who, born in the midst of these debasing associations, grew up to a premature knowledge of evil, and an utter ignorance of any higher code of ethics than the rude life of the miners illustrated.

Young Bullion was not explicit concerning these darker features of his experience. He seemed to avoid details with a sense of shame; and I fancied that the shame was of recent origin, that something had lately aroused him to a perception of the disgrace, and to an odd resolution, not at all like the usual repentance of awakened sinners, to clean the name of the O'Ballyhans. What this cause was I could not gather. He was silent on that point. But, whatever it was, it had made a man of him before his time. He was sixteen years old, though he looked both older and younger. He showed no trace of Irish origin in his talk, which differed from the mixed lingo of the Pacific coast, only in a freedom from coarseness and profanity which evidently cost him some effort. I inferred that this also was a recent change, dating from the time when he had "swore off" from gambling and drinking, and had put his father in the strait-jacket of filial discipline. Of his mother he spoke with a queer, kindly indifference, saying that she "wasn't much account," had no "savey;" but "th' ole man's goin's-on had been rough on her." He regarded his father as an "enfant terrible," an unwelcome responsibility, the management of whom, nevertheless, gave him a certain sense of pleasure in his own skill. "Th' ole man's sharp," he said; "but he ain't no match for me!"

A year before this, the O'Ballyhans, with slender stock of household goods, had emigrated to Pactolus Gulch. It was not a promising field. The placer diggings were nearly exhausted, and the population had nearly all departed. But there was business enough still (there always is) for one liquor-saloon; and in this establishment the elder O'Ballyhan became barkeeper. His taste for whiskey would have made him an unprofitable servant; but his dexterity with cards made him useful to the proprietor, who pitted him against all comers in the fashionable operation of "playing for the drinks." Now that the claims in the Gulch paid so poorly, and dust was not plenty, the gambling of the Pactolus people seldom went beyond these modest stakes; and as O'Ballyhan was allowed to drink only what he could earn in this way, why, the more he drank, the better for the business.

Meanwhile the boy, so far as I could make out, had turned his hand to whatever he could find in the way of occasional occupation. He had been a supernumerary hostler to the stage; he had worked a while in a played-out placer-claim; he had caught trout in the North Fork, above the place where the tailings made it too muddy even for a sucker or an eel; he had hunted quails, rabbits, and gophers, and sometimes deer; once he had shot a grizzly bear.

When he mentioned that experience, I interrupted him to ask for further particulars. "How did I do it?" said he. "I jist walked up within twenty yards of him, 'n shot him in the mouth. He rolled over quiet enough. Yer see, I had Jim Knowles's repeatin' rifle. A grizzly ain't nothin' if yer have a repeatin' rifle, 'n keep cool. 'F that shot hadn't fetched him, there was seven more ready for him; 'n there never was a grizzly that could swaller seven ounce-balls at one mouthful."

With the precarious proceeds of these industries, he had (as I managed to make him own) kept his mother from starvation; and his quick wits and ready helpfulness had evidently moved all the Pactolians to admiration and friendship. He had never taken much to book-learning, having rebelled entirely at a languid attempt of the old man to educate him. "Educate!" said he contemptuously, as he told us about it: "didn't want none o' his kind. Two fellers in one family slingin' Latin, 'n puttin' on the heavy genteel, 'd 'a' been too much gravy for the meat." But I gathered that there was a school now at Pactolus of which he had a very high opinion.

"Do you go?" I asked, forgetting, for the moment, that he was a capitalist, and man of business.

"No," he replied gloomily: "hain't got time. But I walk over there afternoons to see the teacher."

"Is he a very good teacher?"

"It's a lady," he said shortly, and changed the subject, proceeding to tell of the great discovery which had in six months brought fresh life to Pactolus district, and changed the fate of more than one of its inhabitants; namely, the discovery of the Agamemnon lode, and the inauguration thereby of a new era of prosperous activity.

It was the old story, repeated in so many districts on the Pacific coast in early days. Young Bullion had found the outcrop of the lode far above the head of the Gulch, and had pounded up a sack-full of the strange, dark ore, and "panned" it in vain for gold. Disappointed but curious, he had carried a specimen of it to the saloon, and passed it around among the loungers who sat sociably about the red-hot stove. They could make nothing of it. But O'Ballyhan, senior, who was mellow with a day's professional work, had got possession of it, and with drunken eloquence pronounced it to be *lapis philosophorum*, the philosopher's stone ("with a lot of other Latin," added Agamemnon), and finally, seizing the poker for a wand, had opened the door of the stove, tossed the specimen into the blazing fire, and declared himself to be an alchemist engaged in the manufacture of *aurum potabile*. This, at least, is my version of it, based on Young Bullion's attempt to repeat the jargon of his drunken dad. True, the ancient alchemist did not make aurum potabile *in* the fire, but over it; not by fusion, but by solution; but O'Ballyhan was drunk, and so may have departed from the prescription. Nobody cared for his vagaries. Only his son, when the others had departed, raked over the embers to recover his specimen, and found it studded with globules of exuded silver.

He was too shrewd to make immediate outcry over the discovery. For several days he kept it to himself, while he meditated thoroughly his plan of procedure. Then, taking into his counsel a miner who had had some experience in "quartz," he arranged a programme, which was carried out to the letter. A meeting of citizens was held; the startling announcement of the existence of silver veins in the neighborhood was proclaimed; and a code of laws was proposed. The assembly, being fiercely eager to adjourn and go "prospecting," passed the laws in a hurry; and the first location recorded was the Agamemnon. A week later, every chunk or bowlder of rock, in place or out of place, streaked, spotted, black, or white, that showed itself on that mountain-slope, had been "discovered," named, and recorded. A fine crop of litigation and pistol-shooting about disputed titles had been planted. But the title to the Agamemnon no one disputed: its discoverer was the benefactor of the district. The saloon-keeper, deeply impressed by the incident of the stove, advanced five hundred dollars for a fractional interest in the claim; and with this money Young Bullion began operations. But, foreseeing that it would not last long, he called the miners together, and proposed, that, instead of wasting their labor each on his own mine, they should unite to open the Agamemnon to a considerable depth, extract a lot of ore, send it to the Bay, and sell it for the benefit of all parties. This they had done with unexpected success; and Young Bullion had been able to send by express from San Francisco a good round sum for each of them, besides opening the negotiation for the sale of his mine. Meanwhile the news had spread, and the tide of population had turned again to flood. Empty houses were inhabited once more; the hotel was re-opened; "The Weekly Nozzle" (christened in honor of a now defunct hydraulic scheme) began to play again, and talked of expanding into a daily under the title of "The Morning Blast;" and the schoolhouse had once more a teacher.

Listening to Agamemnon's story made the time pass rapidly; and, before we were aware, we were at the next station, where the horses were to be changed, and the passengers fed.

I do not know why I have omitted to mention that the stage was well filled inside, but that the passengers were not a particularly interesting company, with the exception of one, — a singularly intelligent and refined-looking young woman, who had joined us at the last station before that at which I went outside. A new-comer always has a great advantage in such circumstances. Even an ordinary woman, if neatly dressed, and spotless as to collar and cuffs, seems almost a saint or an angel by comparison with a thoroughly dusty load of travel-worn sufferers.

But this lady was not an ordinary person. There was a — what's the use of trying to describe her? I will at least postpone the desperate task; and perhaps the progress of my story may make it unnecessary. Suffice it to say here, that an hour's sitting opposite her in the stage had quite filled my mind with a sort of tender curiosity as to her character, her history, and her errand into the rude society of the Sierra. But Young Bullion, with his quaint and vigorous narrative, had driven out her image.

It returned, however, with fresh force, when we all alighted for dinner, and I hastened gallantly to help her out of the coach, on which occasion, let me say, I observed that her foot and hand were small, while her step and clasp were firm. (There's *so* much of my description unconsciously done for me, thank goodness!)

But surely it was not at sight of me that she blushed, and looked confused? No: it was at some one behind me, to wit, Young Bullion; and, upon my word, he was blushing too, unless his complexion deceived me. The next instant my fair unknown (yes, she was fair: put that down in the description) walked straight up to him, and said in her peculiarly sweet, clear voice (another item), "How do you do, Mr. O'Ballyhan? Have you had a pleasant journey? It is quite an unexpected pleasure to meet you here. I have been spending a day or two visiting some friends in the Valley." [This with a graceful but indefinite gesture, which might indicate any thing from Los Angeles to Chico.] "We have had a little vacation, to get a new floor put in the schoolhouse."

It struck me that she seemed a trifle anxious to answer his possible questions before he asked them. If so, she need not have feared embarrassment from any inquisitiveness on his part. In her presence Young Bullion the capitalist, Agamemnon the ruler of men, was merely an awkward boy. It was all he could do to introduce me, at my request. But style was not important under the circumstances; and I was satisfied when I found myself on a footing of agreeable acquaintance with Miss Mary Carleton, the Pactolus school-teacher.

At the table I managed to improve a good many opportunities in the way of "passing" the potatoes, and such delicacies; and, as Young Bullion closely watched and eagerly imitated these courtesies, I fancy Miss Mary was waited upon as never before.

All the company resumed their places at the accustomed signal; and the rest of the journey passed quietly enough. Agamemnon apparently did not wish to talk, and, as evening approached, rolled himself up and went to sleep again on the upper seat. The shadows deepened in the cañons; and the red evening-glow slipped upward on the hills, and faded out at last from their summits into the sky, where it lingered yet a while before giving place entirely to the starlight.

Stephen and I chatted sedately and at intervals, until the spirit of the time charmed us to silence, and we smoked our pipes in placid revery. At midnight everybody was aroused; for with cracking of whip, and barking of dogs, and clattering of hoofs, and rattling of wheels, we drove up to the Pactolus hotel; and nobody was going any farther. I lodged at the hotel, and saw no more of Young Bullion that night. Tired as I was, I noted, with a slight touch of envy, that he re-entered the stage, for the purpose, as I inferred, of "seeing Miss Mary home."

Next morning, after breakfast, Agamemnon appeared, to "talk business." We walked through the single street of the town, along the edge of the irregular excavation which had been Nature's "gulch," and had become man's "diggin's," until the last house was reached. It was the schoolhouse; and Miss Mary, standing in the doorway, just about to ring the "second bell," waved us a greeting as we passed. (She had a pretty arm, too !) On a little height beyond, we paused, and turned to enjoy the very picturesque prospect of houses and pine-covered hills, great red excavations; busy miners, and rolling foot-hills piled behind and below all

" That's whar the O'Ballyhans live," said my companion, pointing to the house nearest the schoolhouse, — a low, large log-cabin.

" And where does Miss Carleton live ? " I asked.

" She boards with us," he replied curtly, and faced about to resume the march.

The miners of the West have a notion that the richest mines are to be sought in the most inaccessible places. How far this might be recognized, if otherwise stated, as a fact with a scientific reason, I will not stop to explain. At all events, it was true of the Agamemnon, which occupied a very high and very bare mountain-spur of porphyritic rock, belonging properly to a more eastern belt than the granite and slate of the gulch proper. A lower summit and a heavy belt of pine-timber separated this desert height from the settlement. One might say that the characteristic scenery of two States was here brought close together. Nevada peeped over a gap in the edge of the Sierra into California.

I began my examination at once, and soon became satisfied that it was indeed a mine of extraordinary value. How this conclusion was reached I do not need to describe here. But it was only after several visits, and many careful samplings and measurements, that my opinion became definite as well as positive. Even this definite judgment was held in abeyance to await the results of the assays of the samples, to be made at San Francisco.

III.

THE PRODIGAL FATHER.

On this first day we spent but a couple of hours in and about the mine, and then returned to town, where I had accepted an invitation to call on the O'Ballyhans. It was long past the dinner-hour. We had shared the miners' meal at their "boarding-house" on the mountain. As we passed the schoolhouse, the hum of reciting voices told that Miss Mary was at work. Presently we entered the rude mansion of Agamemnon's family.

The door opened directly into a large sitting-room; and, as Young Bullion pushed it open without ceremony, we surprised the paternal O'Ballyhan, sitting before a pine table, and lazily engaged, pipe in mouth, in some sort of solitary game of cards.

"At it again?" said Agamemnon angrily; "'n you hain't copied them papers, neither!"

"*Rem acu tetigisti:* bedad! ye've touched the thing acutely, Aggy, me boy; *et nihil tetigisti quod non ornavisti*, an' ye niver touched any thing that ye didn't adorn. Come, now, that's rather nate, av' ye only understood it." This airy reply was thrown off, like a soap-bubble from a pipe, with a wave of the hand and an affectation of easy unconcern. Nevertheless, the speaker managed with the same gesture to sweep the cards into a drawer; and it was not difficult to see that the theatrical sire was really in awe of his practical son.

The latter paid no attention to the classical effusion with which he had been greeted, but continued sternly, "Been drinkin' too. Look here, ole man, this has got to stop. You hear me!"

"*Vultus est index animi*," responded the awful dad: "sure it's me physiognomy betrays me sowl. *In vino veritas:* I couldn't tell ye a lie, me boy. *Ecce signum!* there's the bottle; *eheu! quantum mutatus ab illo!* an' divil a bit left in it!"

Agamemnon might have proceeded to further inquiry and rebuke; but, suddenly recollecting my presence, he dropped, for the time, the process of family discipline, and introduced me as "the quartz-sharp from San Francisco."

The O'Ballyhan rose with exuberant cordiality, and skipped towards me as if I were his partner in a contra-dance. I despair of depicting him. Imagine a grizzly, rummy, bleared visage, surmounted by a shock of bristling gray hair; a short, fat figure clad in a most dilapidated but once gorgeous, large-figured, flowing dressing-gown, which did not pretend to conceal a very dirty shirt; tight pantaloons of the cut and the pattern that were the rage a score of years ago; and a pair of slippers that flapped the floor at every step: in short, a person without the slightest remaining trace of dandyism. Imagine this being to talk and move with immense affectation of gentlemanly style, and you may gain some conception of the O'Ballyhan. I ought to add that his hands would have been white if they had been clean, and that his pipe was a common, short black "cuddy." His profuse quotations of trite scraps of Latin, usually accompanied by free translations into English with a brogue, added to the bizarre and incongruous effect of his whole appearance.

"*Salve!*" he exclaimed: "ye're welcome to the castle o' the O'Ballyhans. *Non sumus quales eramus:* we're not ourselves at all since we left our swate ancistral hall, *natale solum,* so to spake. But *cœlum non animum mutant:* it's the climate, and not the characther, they change"—

"*Qui trans mare currunt,* who come to Castle Garden," said I, finishing his quotation in his own style.

"*Dies faustus, cretâ notandus!*" exclaimed the old scapegrace, with a gesture as if he would embrace me: "it's a blissed day it is, an' we'll mark it wid chalk; that is to say, wid something better. Sure, Aggy, me boy, ye won't grudge yer old father a glass to mark the day. *Date obolum Belisario:* there's no use translatin' that to ye, ye hard-hearted spalpeen."

The last part of this speech was delivered in an altered tone, caused by a frown and shake of the head from Agamemnon, who at this point turned to leave the room. "Where's Mother?" said he.

"*In partis inferioribus*, it's the back-yard I mane, sittin' in the rockin'-chair wid her *otium cum dignitate* an' a favorite author."

True enough, as Agamemnon opened a door opposite to that by which we had entered, I caught a glimpse of the matron, enjoying the pleasant afternoon air in the manner described. Her rocking-chair was the genuine article, city made, and doubtless hauled, with other household belongings, many a weary mile through one family pilgrimage after another. It bore the scars of age and trouble; but it was still able to rock, though in a somewhat rickety way. Mrs. O'Ballyhan was maintaining this motion by timely application of her toes to the ground, while her eyes were riveted upon a pamphlet, of which I could only see that the cover was yellow. Then the door closed behind Agamemnon, and I was left with the sinful sire.

"It's a foine boy," he began, "but clane spoilt wid consate, an' disrespict o' payrints. *Sequitur patrem haud passibus equis* — he takes after his father, but he can't kape up; and it irritates him. *Non tam Minerva quam Mercurio:* it's business he manes, an' not learnin'. But he wasn't born wid a rale jaynius for business, *non nascitur fit*, — faith that's a nate one too, — an' it's mesilf 'll show him a thing. Business is it? *Negotium? Si negotium quæris circumspice. Siste viator!* Av' ye're travelin' on business, talk wid the O'Ballyhan."

Here he assumed a significant air, which convinced me that he intended some confidential communication. Suspecting at the same time that the tawdry adornments of Latin quotations and misquotations in his discourse were deliberately affected, I said, "Well, Mr. O'Ballyhan, if you have any thing to say about the business on which I am traveling, it is my business to hear you. But we shall save time if we confine ourselves to English."

"*Lex loci*," said the incorrigible scamp, in a final effort to impose upon me: "it's the custom o' the country. These barbarians, *damnati ad metalla*, condimned to work in the mines, so to spake, pretind to talk nothin' but English, an' a voile mess they make o' that too. But *jacta est alea in medias res:* I'll begin wid the business immajitly, an' it's dumb in the dead languages I'll be to plaze ye, till I have the honor to resave ye in Ballyhan Castle, County Clare, wid me complate edition o' the *Auctores Classici ad Usum Delphini* in the bookcase behind our two selves, an' the *amphora*, wid the sugar and the hot wather, on the table afore us."

After all, he seemed to take so much squalid comfort in his Latin, that I was half sorry I had tried to cut it short. But the voice of Agamemnon was heard outside; and the old man had only time to say, "Whisht!" I'll mate ye *sub rosa* (beggin' your pardon) to-night in the little grane-room at the back o' the International saloon, and tell ye what's important, if true (an' true it is); an' in the best of English I'll tell it, on the wurrd of an Oirish jintleman!" Then the door opened, and Agamemnon ushered in his mother.

After making the acquaintance of Mrs. O'Ballyhan, I was lost in wonder, that from such a couple the keen, energetic, and straightforward son could have sprung. It was a clear case of what the philosophers call atavism, — the re-appearance, in some remote descendant, of ancestral qualities which are entirely wanting in the intermediate generations. Doubtless, I reflected, the stimulating atmosphere of this newest New World had developed the dormant germs of character in Young Bullion.

Few words will suffice for Mrs. O'Ballyhan. She was, perhaps, the most utterly negative, washed-out woman I ever met. In all my observation of her I detected only two feelings that had survived the otherwise complete wreck of will and emotion; namely, her appetite for novel-reading, and her admiration for her humbug of a husband. Toward Agamemnon, whose industry and executive ability were the only support of the family, she entertained, apparently, only the mournful sentiment that he was not like his father. I tried once to converse with her on the subject of a sensational romance which she had just been reading, and the result convinced me that she did not remember a word or scene of it. She was like a drunkard, who tastes his liquor only for a brief instant while he swallows it, and can not recall its flavor in his craving for more.

I wondered who cooked and washed, — surely not this mere echo of a woman? — and who maintained the general order of the house, the interior of which was by no means so slovenly in appearance as its nominal master and mistress. Two windows mutely answered my two mental queries. Through one of them I saw John Chinaman carrying an armful of wood to the kitchen; through the other, Miss Mary Carleton, briskly returning from school.

I was curious to see what sort of conversation could come of such a strange mixture of ingredients. Would the O'Ballyhan continue to spout maudlin classics, and his spouse sit in rapt vacuity, with her finger in the place where she had left off reading? Would Agamemnon talk about the mine, which must be Greek to the school-teacher, and the school-teacher discourse concerning topics that must be equally Greek to Agamemnon?

"Greek to Agamemnon!" The whimsical coincidence carried my thought further. Of course Miss Mary would have tact, and would speak with Agamemnon in his own tongue as it were. A superior being like her would know how to come down to the level of half-grown natures. Then I found that I was forgetting the whole race of O'Ballyhans, and thinking with all my might of the pretty school-teacher; and then — the door opened, and she stood like a picture against the background of pine-woods and sky.

She did not enter, but said she was going to the post-office to mail a letter. I offered to accompany her; and she assented graciously, observing, that, as the office was next door to the hotel, it would not take me out of my way. So, making an appointment with Agamemnon for the following morning, I took leave of the O'Ballyhans.

We walked slowly down the street in the slant sunshine. What we said as we walked, I think is hardly worth repetition. Indeed, I remember of it only how hard I tried to be agreeable, and how neatly she foiled my attempts to learn any thing about herself.

After supper, as I sat lazily on the porch, watching a dog-fight in the "middle distance," I became aware of the presence of the O'Ballyhan, who had come from his mansion by the perilous road of the gulch itself to avoid the keen eyes of Agamemnon, or the greetings of tell-tale acquaintances. Everybody knew that he was under filial surveillance, and in process of reform against his will; and there were thoughtless persons who would not have hesitated to ask him, in a too sonorous and repetitious way, whether he had a pass from his son to be out after dark.

"Bedad!" he said in a stage-whisper, as he came suddenly upon me out of the shadows, "it's hard worrk I had to lave 'em behind, *domus et placens uxor*, an' thim sharp eyes o' the school-misthress an' me firrst-borrn. Av' they hadn't fell a-talkin' wid wan another, *actum est de Republica*, it would 'a' been all up wid the O'Ballyhan. But I gev 'em the slip; an'. the O'Ballyhan kapes his worrd — *non sine pulvere*, not widout a dale o' throuble. Sure I came widin an ace of findin' meself paddlin' about *in gurgite vasto* in the ould hydthraulic reservoir. A 'rare swimmer' I'd 'a' been — an' that's a nate thing too, 'av' ye comprehind it!"

I was in no mood for the old fellow's discursive conversation, and I brought him peremptorily to business. Thereupon he led the way to the neighboring saloon, and, entering by a back-door, showed me into a room of considerable size, in which a motley crowd was gathered about a green-baize-covered table, intent upon gambling. No one paid attention to us; although the O'Ballyhan, following an impulse which he could not resist, paused at the table, and stood on tiptoe, to watch the game over the shoulders of the players.

"Maybe ye'd loike to try yer luck," he whispered. "*Audaces fortuna juvat*, the bould boy's the lucky wan! Or ye moight make use o' my supayrior skill an' expayrience, by permittin' me the honor to invist a small amount for ye?"

I shook my head sternly, and motioned him away.

"Ah, thin, it's a comforthable drop ye'd prefer. *Ad utrumque paratus* — the O'Ballyhan's ready to accommodate ye." He withdrew me to a small table in a remote corner, and, disappearing for a moment, returned with two glasses full of some variety of alcoholic "mixed drink," such as the seasoned palates of Pactolus required. When I declined to join him, he proceeded in due course to perform duty for both of us, and, as I found afterwards, at my expense. ("D'ye think," said the barkeeper forcibly, "that we'd 'a' trusted that old galoot for half a dozen drinks, if he hadn't ordered for a respectable gent?")

After all these preliminaries, he began to develop his important communication. It was twofold: first, he wanted to bribe me; secondly, he tried to blackmail my clients through me. He had the power to destroy the value of the title to the Agamemnon lode, and would use it if he were not bought off. To this I replied, "Very well. If there is any such trouble about the title, I shall advise my clients to have nothing to do with it, and of course I shall tell your son the ground of my unfavorable decision."

At this he began to weep, with whisky and emotion, and lapsed into Latin, from which his strictly business communication had been comparatively free. "*Est quædam flere voluptas*, there's a certain relayf in tares," quoth he: "*hinc illæ lachrymæ*. But ye wouldn't tell the boy, now, *nec prece nec pretio*, not for love nor money. Sure, he'd murther me." And, in his dismay over this prospect, he abandoned his plan of operations, and confessed that his claim to the title of the mine consisted merely in the fact that Agamemnon was a minor, and that he was consequently himself the real owner. After which I had to help him home.

As I turned away from his door, with his "*Serus in cœlum redeas,* may ye live a thousand yares, an' spind all yer avenin's in improvin' conversation wid the O'Ballyhan!" sounding in my ears, I saw through a window Miss Mary Carleton in her own room. She sat, pen in hand, with a half-written letter before her. Her face was raised, and her eyes were turned upward. Was she thinking of some absent friend, or only hunting after a suitable adjective? I know not; but I know that she had a beautiful profile.

IV.

THE SCHOOL-TEACHER.

I FELT it my duty, on the following day, to call Young Bullion's attention to the possible defect in his title to the mine which bore his name. He chuckled with a knowing air, and, instead of replying to the point, at once began to tease me about my interview with his father.

"Th' ole man show ye how to play cards?"

"No: I didn't choose to learn."

"Stuck ye for the drinks, hey? I knowed it when I see yer towin' him home."

"For *his* drinks. Yes: I must confess I was obliged to pay for them, or make trouble. But how did you happen to see us? I thought you were all abed, except Miss Carleton. There was a light in her room."

"Oh! I was jest prowlin' around, 'n thinkin' matters over — who does she keep a-writin' to, 'n stoppin,' 'n cryin'? That's what I want ter know!" he added fiercely.

With sublime virtue I replied that I didn't know, and that perhaps it was none of our business.

"Ke-*rect*," said Young Bullion: "it's none 'o yours. But it's *my* business when she cries, now, you bet! She ain't a-goin' to cry if Agamemnon O'Ballyhan can help it."

"Who is she?" I inquired.

"Ain't a man in this camp as knows. She jest come down on the camp out o' the sky, 's ef she was sent. Ye see, when things got livelier, on account o' the quartz, the boys said we orter start up the schoolhouse agin. Some on 'em was for havin' church too, right away; said it looked more like civ'l'zation: 'n the others said no, they couldn't afford to run a fustclass parson, an' they warn't goin' to have no cheap sardine of a parson to bring the gospel into contempt. Nor they couldn't agree on the kind o' church, to begin with. Some of 'em up 'n said they was

Catholics, an' some was Methodists, 'n so on; 'n, afore the meetin' that we had to consider the question come to ajourn, there was a dozen religions a-cussin' one another, where nobody knowed, up to that time, there was ary one. So they broke up in a row; 'n the next day a committee come round to me, 'n said the camp was goin' to leave it to me, 'cause my head was level, 'n I hadn't got no prejudices.

"'Well, gentlemen,' says I, 'yer wrong thar: ye hain't allowed for curiosity. I never was inside of a church while she was in operation; 'n I'm o' good mind to give it a trial. But we'll wait 'n see how the mines turn out, 'n we'll get the school to producin' reg'lar, 'n at the same time we can prospect around, 'n stake out for a church.' Then they had another meeting, 'n 'lected me chairman o' the committee on education 'n religion. Th' ole man, he thought he'd got a soft thing, 'n was going to be principal o' the academy. But I sot on *him*. 'N in a day or two along come Miss Carleton, 'n said she was a candidate. Well, we hed a meetin' o' the committee, 'n they asked her fur her references; 'n she give one o' her looks, ye know, 'n said right out, straight 'n clear, 'Gentlemen,' says she, 'fur reasons o' my own, I don't propose to give references. I have taught school in the States, 'n I think I am competent. If you will give me a trial, you will soon find out whether I can manage and teach the children.'

"French Joe, he was on the committee, 'n he objected. But somebody said how would *he* like to furnish references, 'n he shut up quick. 'N Miss Carleton turned round 'n spoke about a dozen words to him in his own lingo,— clear French; 'n Joe was unanimous for her after that, you bet! Well, the more they talked, the more they liked her; 'n at last they voted her in. Now there ain't a man in Pactolus that wouldn't go through fire 'n water to serve her."

"Then, since your school is so well provided for," said I, "you are about ready to start a church."

"I ain't no jedge o' that," responded Young Bullion; "but I guess our boys'd rather hev things as they are. You see, Miss Carleton has half the camp up to the schoolhouse every Sunday afternoon to her Bible-readin's; 'n the boys spend a good part o' the forenoon fixin' up 'n gettin' ready, 'n that keeps 'em out o' mischief. Besides, nobody'd want to go to Bible-readin' *tight:* so they jist haul off early Saturday night, 'nstead o' keepin' 't up all night 'n all Sunday. 'N they set round there till dark, talkin' an' thinkin' it over; 'n what she says jest stays by a feller. Somebody sort o' mentioned the church business the other day, 'n all he got was to dry up: what was the use o' leasin' a priest, 's long 's we had one o' the Lord's own angels free?"

Agamemnon's eloquence on this subject might have continued indefinitely; but I remembered my duty to my employers, and reminded him that the serious question of title ought to be settled immediately, since, without a satisfactory basis in that particular, I could not properly spend time and labor in examining the mine.

"Oh!" said he, "that's all right. The ole man don't git ahead o' me! Why, he was a-copyin' the papers yesterday; 'n when he found that one of 'em was a full deed o' his right, title, 'n interest, he thought he'd struck it rich. Didn't know he hed any right, title, 'n interest up to that time. 'N he hain't, accordin' to the laws o' this district. But I jest got a p'int or two through my agent in San Francisco, so as to make things all serene; 'n when he said the lawyers said that wards, minors, 'n idjits, 'n so forth, couldn't give deeds, says I, ' Who's an idjit? '—' Oh! ' says he, ' it's a minor you are.'—' What kind of a minor,' says I, ' if I can't sell a mine ?' But James he wa'n't no slouch. He understood it right up to the handle; 'n he explained it all, 'n we got the papers fixed before I left."

"But perhaps your father will refuse to sign, unless you pay him some of the money."

"He won't sign, won't he?" said Young Bullion with superb contempt. "He'd sign away his ole soul for five dollars, or one dollar, or two bits; 'n he'll sign that thar deed for nothin' when I tell him to."

"You seem to be very confident of your power over him. Do you use corporal punishment in the family?" I asked jocosely.

He took my question quite in earnest. "I know what you mean," said he: "we had a talk about that in the school committee; 'n Miss Carleton said she wouldn't hev it. But it's a hefty thing to fall back on. As to *my* family, I never had to lick th' old man but once; but I did it up in style that time. He was bangin' th' ole woman about the room; 'n I made up my mind if he couldn't set a better example 'n that, I'd commence 'n boss the shebang myself. But I've got a better holt on him than that. Don't you worry: he'll sign."

I suspected afterwards, no matter on what evidence, that the son had saved the father from either lynching or jail by paying some claim, which, if pressed, would have convicted the old scamp of felony; and that he now held *in terrorem* over the culprit's head, for purposes of reform, the proofs of the crime. What a strange feeling he must have entertained towards a father whom he could make such sacrifices to save, and then govern by a mixture of thrashing and blackmail! Young Bullion's code of ethics was certainly confused. He seemed to have a sense that the family was a burden laid on him by fate, to be borne without complaining, and a fierce determination, that, though it was a burden, it should cease to be a disgrace.

My examination of the mine and neighborhood was prolonged through that week and the next. I sent off very early, however, my preliminary report and a box of samples by express, with a letter to my clients, saying that I would await further advices, and watch the developments of the work then going on. This was no doubt wise: but I was conscious that circumstances made it also pleasant; for, as the days went on, I became, in every respect except her own personal history, very well acquainted with Miss Carleton. We had many subjects of conversation which she could not discuss with the rude inhabitants of Pactolus. She possessed the great charm of directness and simplicity. Perfectly aware of the worshiping regard of her constituency, she spoke of it as openly, and yet with as little vanity (or affected modesty, which is the same thing), as if it were another person, and not herself, that was concerned. "It is a great pleasure," she said one day, "to be really a 'superior being,' and to go down to help and lift such thankful souls as these. There is a sort of intoxication about it — for a young woman of twenty-one."

"Do you never feel a longing for some companionship more congenial, — more like what you have been accustomed to?"

"I did; and I am grateful to you for taking so much interest in my work, giving me such intelligent sympathy."

I felt a little guilty at this; for my interest in the work was certainly subordinate to my interest in the woman. Our acquaintance, however, remained on the same footing as at first. I wondered why I could not even assume the fraternal tone. When she was sad, as I often fancied she was, why did she so effectively evade sympathy, saying, "Now I am tired and melancholy, don't mourn with me, but make me laugh?" And why —

Well, thus I drifted, until it was high time for me to stop wondering over her position, and take an observation as to my own. But everybody knows that it may be high time for some duty, and yet one may take no note of the time until some signal sounds the hour. At last the clock struck for me.

On the second Saturday a letter arrived from my clients, advising me that the results of all assays had been favorable beyond my estimates, and that, if my own judgment continued to approve the purchase, they would close the bargain at once. I was instructed to see that the papers were made out in due form, and Mr. O'Ballyhan could then express them to his agent in San Francisco, who could deliver them, and receive the money.

I went at once to Young Bullion, half expecting that this good news would startle him out of his preternatural maturity. It would have been a relief to hear him whoop with joy, or see him stand on his head. But he turned pale, and staggered as if he had been shot.

"It's 'most too much for me," he said; "not the money, but" —

With an effort that gave me a higher conception

than ever of his manly self-control, he turned hastily to the table-drawer, and produced the papers of title. They were complete in every particular, — the certificate of original location, the deeds of the co-locators to Agamemnon Atrides O'Ballyhan, the complete and absolute quit-claim of Miles O'Ballyhan and Leonora his wife, to the said Agamemnon, — all duly acknowledged and indorsed by the proper officer, as recorded in the proper "Liber." The young man had evidently not been idle. He must have ridden to the county-seat, many miles away, to secure these last, and in those days somewhat unusual, evidences of regularity. The papers were all in the same handwriting, — an elaborate, flourishing script, which he said was the old man's. Finally he showed me another deed, transferring the title in blank, and not yet signed. "When I put my name to that," said he, "the thing's drove in 'n clinched. I left this one blank; because, if your folks didn't buy, I might want to use it for some one else."

"I find every thing in order," I replied. "You have only to fill up and execute this final deed, and send it to your agent."

Then I walked out, and up into the woods, and meditated for a long time upon non-professional matters, without coming to any conclusion.

Should I seek a final interview with Miss Carleton? and, if so, what should I say to her? I was not so really "in love" as to deliberately intend to offer myself to her without knowing any thing of her history; yet I felt that a farewell talk might lead me to just that rash act, unless I definitely decided beforehand what should be its nature.

My reflections were suddenly interrupted by the appearance of the lady herself. Since it was Saturday afternoon, and therefore holiday, she was evidently intending to use her freedom for a walk. Ordinarily I would have hastened to join her, with a pleasant impression that my company was not unwelcome. This time, however, I hesitated; because I had not yet finished my mental debate, and was in a perilous state of impressible uncertainty. I remained sitting a little distance from the path, in the expectation that she would pass by without seeing me; then, I thought, I would hasten to make up my mind, and on her return I could casually meet her, prepared to speak as the result of my reflection might dictate. I ought to add that prudence would have had, in any case, nothing to say if I had been able to see any signs of a more than friendly interest on her part; but I could not honestly say to myself that any such sign had been discernible hitherto. I could not doubt that a declaration of any special interest on my part would be a great surprise to her; and really, I was not myself prepared to make it, unless hurried over the edge of deliberation by some sudden impulse.

She neither saw me nor passed me: on the contrary, she stepped aside from the path, and seating herself on a fallen tree a few yards in front of me, and with her back to me, read and re-read a letter; then, looking steadfastly down over the town, and out through the gulch, toward the foot-hills and the valley, she seemed to be weeping. Which would be more embarrassing? — to make my presence known, or to remain an involuntary witness of her suffering? I had just resolved to go forward and speak to her — any words that would comfort her — when a new incident checked my purpose. Headlong up the path came Mr. Agamemnon Atrides O'Ballyhan. There was no indecision about *his* manner. He came, to use a homely comparison, "as if he had been sent for."

V.

NOT MISS MARY — BUT " QUITE CONTRAIRY."

A MOMENT more, and he stood before Miss Carleton. " I saw ye goin' up the hill," he said breathlessly, " 'n I thought I'd catch yer. The Agamemnon's sold, Miss Mary: she's sold!"

With ready sympathy, putting aside her own trouble, she replied, " How glad I am! Now what will you do?"

"That's what — what I was a-goin' to ask y' about. Ye see, I s'pose th' ole man 'n Mother ought to be fixed somehow; ought to be took care of, I mean. Not to have any money: they can't take care o' money. Ye see, he'd spend it in cards 'n whisky, 'n she'd spend it in novels and opium. Gets opium on the sly from the Chinamen. Now, I mean to ap-pint Cripple Dan gardeen for them two. He'll never do no more work since the bank caved in on him; but he is smart enough to watch 'em, 'n not be took in by any o' their tricks. He can play cards with th' ole man to keep him out o' gamblin', 'n he can buy novels as fast as Mother can swaller 'em. Shouldn't wonder if he could ring in some o' th' old ones on her once in a while, by changin' the covers. But whisky 'n opium — they must be kep' out."

"A very practical arrangement, I should say. But what are *you* going to do?"

At this simple question Young Bullion became much embarrassed. "Do you," said he, "Miss Mary — would you — is seventy-five thousand dollars enough, do you think, to run a reg'lar gentleman's house?"

She sighed involuntarily. "It is enough to maintain a happy home with every comfort and luxury. There are many refined 'gentlemen' who bring up their families in content on far less money than the income of that sum."

"Well, but — Miss Mary — would it be enough for *you*?"

She started in astonishment. "For *me*? What do you mean?"

"I mean," replied the young man, conquering his timidity, and speaking with a simple dignity that made him handsome, — "I mean that you are the one that made me want to be a gentleman, 'n I can't be a gentleman unless you help me; 'n I love the ground you tread on, Miss Mary. If you'll be my wife, you shall never work, or cry, or be sorry again."

There was a moment of painful silence. Then she said, "I did not dream of this. I am so much older than you, you know."

"You are not so very much older," he pleaded. "That is not what troubled *me*. But you are so much better 'n wiser, that's what's the matter with you! I wouldn't 'a' dared to speak to ye; but I knowed ye was in trouble. 'N now the Agamemnon's sold, 'n what's it all good for, 'f I can't give it to you?"

"My dear friend," she answered slowly, but with that simple frankness which belonged to her, "I have been — I am — in trouble; but I can not take your help. You must forget, as I will forget, all that you have said, but not the kindness that prompted it, nor the gratitude with which I refuse it."

Agamemnon looked keenly at her, with the air of one who still pursued a fixed purpose. The refusal of his offer did not seem to be a conclusive defeat to his mind.

"Ye couldn't change yer mind?" he asked reflectively.

"No."

"Not never? Not if I was older'n I be?"

"Never. You must not think of it."

"Then ye're married to some other feller!" said Agamemnon, with a sad triumph. "Now, Miss Mary, it ain't no business o' mine, I know; but ye'd better tell me, anyhow. Wouldn't it sort o' quiet my mind, 'n do me good, hey?"

This subtle appeal to her benevolence accomplished what no inquisitive stratagem could have compassed. After a slight hesitation she said, "There is not much to tell, and it is not very important that I should keep it secret, only I have preferred to do so; and I trust you to help me in that. Yes, I am married; and my dear husband is slowly recovering at — at a place on the San Joaquin, from a long, wasting fever. I left him when he was pronounced out of danger, and I have seen him but once since then. It was the other day, when I took the journey by stage from which I returned on the same coach with you. It is hard to be parted from him."

"Now, don't ye cry again, Miss Mary. It ain't none o' my business, ye know; but it would sort o' settle my mind — he's good to ye, ain't he? Ye didn't go for to leave him 'cause he wouldn't let ye boss the ranch?"

"The ranch?" she replied sadly. "I left him because, after his long illness, we were so poor that we were in danger of losing our pretty ranch altogether, and of starving perhaps, unless one of us could get work. That one was I; and the work I understand best is teaching."

"You bet!" assented Young Bullion with enthusiasm. "But — jest to ease my mind completely, ye know — why didn't you tell somebody afore? This camp would 'a' raised yer salary, 'n fetched yer husband up here, 'n built ye a shebang, 'n — look here, what line o' business is he in?"

"He is a minister."

"Whoop la!" shouted Young Bullion: "that's our lay exactly. There's a fust-class vacancy right here, 'n I'll — no, I guess I couldn't quite stand it, hevin' him around: that's what's the matter with *me!* But why didn't you tell us afore this — this trouble was made? We'd 'a' voted him 'n you in unanimous. Anybody that's a good 'nough husband fer you 's a good 'nough minister fer us."

"I wish I had told you all at the beginning," said she; "but, perhaps, if I had done so, you would have declined my services altogether. I heard about your dispute over a minister, and I feared to let you know I was a minister's wife. It was so important, so very important to me then, to get a place immediately."

Young Bullion made no reply. If what he had heard had not "eased his mind," it had at least given him much to think about. The silence which ensued recalled me to a sense of my embarrassing position as a listener; and, with sudden presence of mind, I stepped forward.

"You must pardon me, my friends," I said, "that I have overheard your conversation. Nothing that you have said shall be repeated. But every word has deepened my respect for both of you. If I can in any way be of service to you, Mrs. — Mrs. Mary, you have only to command me as a faithful friend." Then I lifted my cap, and retired in as good order as a fellow could — under the circumstances.

I had gone but a few steps when Young Bullion overtook me. That boy's penetration was most annoying at times, and this was one of the times.

"Goin' to play fer the school-teacher yerself, wa'n't ye, if I hedn't got the call fust?" was his dreadful greeting. "Well, 'tain't no use fer nary one of us. You jest go 'n thank the Lord y'ever knowed her, 'n don't you whine 'cause she's picked out a better man. No cryin' over spilt milk. That's *me!*" And he straightened himself until his short stature visibly increased.

I got rid of Young Bullion as soon as practicable, and went to the hotel in a dazed condition, as if I had fallen from the top of the mountain, and rolled down the gulch. When one has seriously weighed a question like that which had occupied my thoughts that afternoon, it is inevitably startling to find that it was a matter wholly beyond question all the time. I wanted to think it over. But I did not succeed in thinking it over on the porch after supper: so I went to bed to meditate there; and finally I went to sleep, my last reflection being, that I would review the whole matter on the morrow, after which I would pay the school-teacher a cordial, friendly farewell call.

But the morrow brought its own topics for surprise and reflection. At early dawn I was waked by a hand on my shoulder, and, turning sleepily in bed, met the energetic look of Agamemnon Atrides O'Ballyhan. He, at least, had thought over his situation, and made his decision.

"Sorry to h'ist ye so early," said he; "but I'm off. Now, don't ye go fer to ask no questions, but 'tend to business. Here's them papers: they're all right, 'n you'll find my directions along with 'em. I'm off. Take care o' yerself, ole boy." And he was gone.

I opened the package he had left on my bed. It contained all the papers I had previously inspected. The final deed, however, had been filled up and executed; and I was not a little surprised to find my own name inserted as the new owner of the Agamemnon. Enclosed in the deed, however, was a document in a cramped schoolboy hand which threw full light on the transaction. It ran as follows:—

"This is my Will But I aint ded no nor goin to be but I am as good as ded wich it is All the Same Ime gon over the Range the mine belongs to miss mary and u give her the munny she knos about Criple dann and the olman and mother you pay my agent 1 thousn Dolars and doan take nothin for yureself yure foaks pays u with the munny i antid up i truss u becaus u likt miss mary too.

"AGAMEMNON ATRIDES O'BALLYHAN."

Why should I detain the reader with an account of what followed? It was not easy for me to execute the charge confided to me. The lady at first utterly refused to accept the strange legacy of which I was trustee. But I succeeded in persuading her to take the money, and carry out Agamemnon's wishes until he should be found, — an event which I felt sure he would not permit to happen. "Get your husband to come here and live," I said. "If the boy ever means to be seen again, it is to this place he will come; and it is here, in the good work you have begun, of which his own awakened manhood was one of the first-fruits, that you should expend the income of his legacy."

Cripple Dan, it turned out, had been already sounded as to his willingness to take charge of the two wayward O'Ballyhans on a handsome allowance for the three. He assumed the position at once, and smashed two hidden bottles for the O'Ballyhan the first day. That disconsolate old toper supposed the orders for this vandalism proceeded from the school-teacher. "*Dux fœmina facti*, it's a woman is in it: *cedant arma togæ*, the glory o' the O'Ballyhans is swipt away be a petticoat," was his lament. But he submitted to be made comfortable, and seemed none the worse for his enforced sobriety.

VI.

SIMILIA SIMILIBUS CURANTUR.

Thus I left them all, and closed a chapter in my own life which I expected never to re-open. But time brings about unexpected coincidences; and what should it bring to me, the other day, ten years after the events narrated in this story, but a visit from Agamemnon Atrides O'Ballyhan? — a prosperous, manly fellow as one would wish to see, with stylish clothes and a fine mustache. And on his arm — could I believe my eyes? Was it the school-teacher, become as much younger as Agamemnon had grown older?

"Mrs. O'Ballyhan," said he proudly, "Miss Mary's sister. You and I didn't feel very happy that day, you know; but now I'm glad I waited." The latter remark was fortunately an aside, so that Mrs. O'Ballyhan did not hear it.

"You bet!" I answered, clothing due felicitation in what I thought would be congenial style. But I was mistaken as to the style. Agamemnon had "swore off" from slang so far as human nature would permit. Only now and then, as he confessed, "conversation got the better of him."

During the short half-hour that the happy pair sat in my office, my old friend gave me an outline of his career from the day when we had parted. It would make another story by itself, and I am sorry that it must be condensed in a few lines.

After "striking it rich" again, over the Range in Nevada, and accumulating from several lucky hits a fortune at least double that which he had given away, he had returned to Pactolus six years from the day of his disappearance.

"It took me about that time," said he, "to get over things. But then I couldn't rest till I had seen the old place, and so I came back. The old folks were both dead — best thing for 'em. But there was the minister and his wife just about worshiped by everybody; and there was an Agamemnon Academy, and an Agamemnon Free Library, and so on, all built with the interest of my money. You'd better believe everybody was astonished to see me. All thought I was dead, sure, except Miss Mary: she stuck to it I would come back. Even when they found somebody's bones over in the sage-brush beyond the summit, and had a funeral on 'em, she wouldn't let 'em call my name at the funeral, nor put it on the tombstone.

"Well, they wanted me to take back my capital. But I told 'em I'd got enough; and, at any rate, there wasn't any hurry. I'd stay round a while, and consider. So, after I had considered a little, I went to Miss Mary and the parson, and says I, 'What I want is to go to school. I feel pretty old; but I guess I ain't too old to learn.' You see, my Susy here, she was assistant teacher in the academy, and I thought she could teach me if anybody could. But they said I was too big to go and sit on the benches in the academy. Susy said she couldn't think of trying to manage a scholar twenty-two years old: that was so *very* old,— a whole year older than she was! So I had to take up with the minister's offer to give me private instruction. And I got my pay, too, before long; for the minister said I got ahead so fast that I had better join the reading-class. That meant to come every other day and read and talk over books with him and his wife and Susy.

"It was a good while before I made up to Susy. Had a good lesson once, you know — and, besides, I had got more bashful. The more I learned, the more I found I didn't know; and I felt so ugly and clumsy, and inferior every way, it didn't seem as if a lady like her would care for me — unless it was by reason of the two hundred thousand dollars. But Susy didn't know about that, and she wouldn't have minded it a mite if she had. Fact is, she thought a good deal better of me than I deserved all the time; for her folks had been cracking me up for years and years, and all the Academy Commencements and the Annual Reports had a lot in 'em about the 'munificent founder' and the 'generous benefactor,' and I don't know what all; and so, when I turned up alive at last, she was prepared to believe I was better than

I looked. Anyhow, I got to be like one of the family; and Susy was as good as she could be, and took no end of pains with me, to help me put on a little style, and talk the correct thing, and so on. And one day she was showing me how to hold yarn for her to wind; and says I, sitting there as meek as a lamb, 'Seems to me, if you couldn't manage a big boy of twenty-two, you've somehow got the knack of managing him now he's nigh twenty-four.'

"Well, one thing led to another; and that skein of yarn got so tangled (because I forgot to lay it down), that Susy said it should never be unraveled. She keeps it as a curiosity.

"The next morning I went to the parson, and says I, 'Now let's talk business. I'll take that hundred thousand back, just to please you; though I've got twice as much, and I don't want it.' He said, 'All right;' but he looked a little cast down too. Parsons are human.

"'Now,' says I, 'it's mine; and I'm going to make another business proposition. You marry Susy and me, and I'll give you, say, a hundred thousand dollars as a wedding-fee.'

"'Oho!' says he. 'Well, my boy; she's worth it. You've made a good bargain, and so have I.'

"That was two years ago; and Susy and I have just been the happy pair you read about, ever since. She's been going right ahead with my education, and got about as much polish on me, I guess, as the grain will bear. You can't make mahogany out o' redwood, if you rub it for ever. So the other day I made a little turn in Agamemnon stock,— those blamed fools in California Street thought the mine was played out, when they had a new body of first-class ore right under their noses,— and I asked Susy if she didn't think a little foreign travel was about the thing to finish off with. She wasn't long saying yes to that; and here we are, bound for everywhere. I expect we'll go round the world before we stop."

We had a most friendly and familiar chat; and the last I heard of them was as they were departing in merry mood together, and the sweet voice of Mrs. O'Ballyhan said, "He offered to get the Legislature to change it; but I said No. I like him just as he is, name and all— Agamemnon Atrides O'Ballyhan."

She laughed a musical laugh of mingled mirth and pride as she added, glancing fondly at her husband, "But I call him 'my dear,' for short."

WIDOW BAKER:

A NEW-ENGLAND STORY.

CHAPTER I.

SQUIRE AND DEACON.

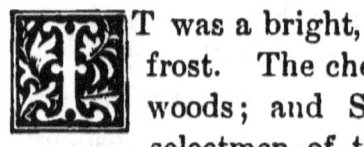T was a bright, still day, after the first hard frost. The chestnuts were dropping in the woods; and Squire Hawkins, one of the selectmen of the town of Hucklebury, was burning brush on his side-hill ten-acre-lot. The squire had got through with the heavy work, and had nothing to do but to watch the fire while he tinkered here and there at the fence. So, when Deacon Peabody's white horse, pulling a shay with the deacon in it, came in sight on the hill-road, the squire had no reason to deny himself the expectation of a comfortable and leisurely chat. From where he stood, he could see the turnpike that came from the corners and went through the valley, past the red school-house, and past Westcott's sawmill, to Hucklebury

Center and South Hucklebury, and so on to larger places. And when he saw the deacon's shay turn from the pike and begin to ascend the hill-road, he knew that in about fifteen minutes the deacon would be at hand. That gave him time to fix up one more length of fence, and to fold his arms sociably on the top-rail, ready for an interview. The deacon's horse stopped opposite the squire, without needing any hint from his driver. He knew the custom of the country, and was not averse to it, particularly when the opportunity to observe it occurred on a convenient, level spot, at the end of a steep pull.

"Wal, Deacon," said the squire heartily, "I'm glad to see ye out agin. We've kind o' missed ye at meetin', 'n everywhere else too, for that matter. The parson, he says he's all lost o' Sundays 'thout you to look at: dunno whether he's been s'fficiently explicit on a tough pint o' doctrine, or not. You took it most too hard, Deacon. Grief is nateral, of course, to a reasonable extent; but Mis' Peabody had been a-failin' so long, ye know; and it was a gret marcy she passed away comfortable in body an' mind; an', on the hull, there's much to be thankful for. I expect it *is* kind o' lonesome, now she's gone;" and the squire paused, with the air of one who had administered consolation and rebuke in wise proportions.

Deacon Phineas Peabody took no offense where none was meant. He had nursed his invalid wife through her long illness, — an old-fashioned, slow consumption, — and he had shut himself up for a month after her death, in a silent sorrow too deep for words; but now he had braced himself again for the duties of life, and he quite assented to the rough but well-meant observations of his friend.

"Yes," said the deacon meditatively, "she lasted a good while; 'n I dunno's I ever quite giv' up hopin' about her. She'd git a little better some weeks, 'n then agin a little wuss; 'n *she* was allers lookin' on the dark side herself, so *I* sort o' got in the way o' s'posin' mebbe she wa'n't so bad's she thought for. Them last drops that her sister Mahaly sent up from Boston seemed to take right hold of her cough. But it wa'n't no use: it was ordained. Cynthy was right, after all. I s'pose the Lord kind o' prepared her for what was comin'."

"There's Susan," said the squire. "She must be gret comfort to ye. She's a good gal, Susan is. I've follered her ever sence she was a little bit of a thing, comin' over to our house after maple-sugar. I used to think young Jotham Baker and she would make a match on't; but, bless you! these young folks will hev their own idees, and they're too sharp for us old fellows to find 'em out. I tell ye, I was jest up-an'-down mortified when Jotham came to me, an' told me he was engaged to Westcott's darter Nancy. Not but she was a nice gal, 'n I had nothin' agin the match, except that old Westcott was a Methodist 'n a Democrat, 'n it did seem kind o' mean to hold Nancy responsible for that. But I thought, after all his goin's on with Susan, it wasn't jest exactly right for him to go off arter another one; 'n I told him so. Says I, 'Jotham, my boy, there ain't no objection to your takin' a wife, in the fear o' the Lord, wherever you find her, amongst the Moabites, or the Hittites, or the Methodists, or the Democrats; but I don't like this philanderin' at the same time with Susan Peabedy.' Jotham, he bust out a-larfin', 'n says he, 'Why, Susan has know'd all about it ever sence it began. Thet's what I talk about to Susan,' says he. 'Well,' says I, 'it's none o' my business, you know, Jotham: you hevn't got to answer to me for your doin's; but I'd like to know how long ago it began.'

"Wal, he was ready enough to talk about it. He'd 'a' talked all day if I'd 'a' let him. You see, I was an old friend of his fam'ly, 'n Widder Baker sot a good deal by my advice; 'n Jotham, he was like a son to me. So he told me he had been acquainted with Nancy Westcott ever sence the quiltin' down to Westcott's, jest afore last year's donation-party. 'Do tell!' says I, tol'ble scornful; ''n you've know'd Susan Peabody all your life. You must excuse me for sayin' of it, young man; but Susan is wuth a dozen of her.'

"'Susan is the best girl that ever lived,' says he, 'exceptin' Nancy; but that's a very different matter.

I tell ye, Susan wouldn't look at me, onless as a friend.' So off he went, 'n that's a'most the last time I see him. He sailed for the East Injees that fall, 'n now it's about two year, 'n he hain't been heerd from. I've hed it on my mind many a time to tell ye about that talk; ''cause,' says I to myself, 'perhaps the deacon hed the same idee as I did, 'n he might think strange on it that Jotham Baker got engaged, afore he sailed, to Nancy Westcott, arter he'd been payin' attentions to Susan Peabody.'"

The deacon had listened to the squire's voluble story in an absent-minded way, paying, in truth, very little attention to it. He had never quite realized that his little Susan had come to be a young woman. To him she was a dutiful and comely daughter, deeply but not demonstratively loved, a brisk housekeeper, a skillful nurse to her invalid mother, a melodious singer in the choir, and a great favorite with the Widow Baker. Since his wife's death, he had thought more about Susan; and now the squire's allusion to her aroused a host of feelings and reminiscences, in which the love-affairs of Jotham Baker had not the remotest share.

"Exactly," said the deacon, — *not* very exactly, so far as a logical reply was concerned. "Susan's a good darter, 'n a middlin' manager. She used to be a bright, healthy-lookin' gal; but I think it has wore on her, tendin' to her ma. She ain't so spry as she was, 'n the color is kind o' faded out of her cheeks. I'm afeared she's a-goin' to be delicate. Fact is, I was jest ridin' over to Widder Baker's to talk to her about Susan. I thought mebbe she'd fix her up suthin' to take, that'd do her good, 'n set her up. Susan mopes 'n reads too much; though I dunno 's she slights her housekeepin' any. But she's a gret hand for books — takes after her ma. But she won't never be sech a woman as her ma was. Miss Baker was a gret friend o' my Cynthy "

The deacon's simple admiration of his deceased wife would have been amusing, if it had not been pathetic. Probably nobody else would have extolled the intellect of the late Mrs. Peabody; and certainly nobody would have dreamed of pronouncing Susan her inferior, — Susan, who talked on terms of equality with the parson and the doctor and the schoolmaster, and who had even written poetry which had been published with editorial commendation in " The Advertiser." But to the patient and apparently prosaic deacon, there never had come an end of the romantic admiration with which he had in his youth regarded his Cynthia. Indeed, his present visit to the Widow Baker, undertaken on the pretext of talking about Susan, was really inspired by the longing to talk about his wife with one who had known and loved her.

CHAPTER II.

THE STORY OF THE BAKERS.

"Goin' over to Widder Baker's, be ye?" answered the squire. "'Xpect ye hain't heerd the news. Lawyer Marigold, over to the Center, has foreclosed on that Baker mortgage; 'n it's likely Widder Baker'll be turned out o' house 'n home. I was over to the Center yesterday to see what could be done about it. Marigold, he was reasonable enough; didn't want nothin' but his money, an' he's waited for that this ten year, not wishin' to disturb the fam'ly. Ye see, the kernel borrowed the money. Kernel Baker was a well-meanin' man; but all his geese was swans, an' he was shif'less besides, — allers a-contrivin' suthin, or inventin' suthin, 'n never reelly amountin' to nothin'. There was that patriotic warfle-iron o' his'n, — in the shape of the American eagle. He was sure he had got a fortin' in that. Fact is, I thought it was a good idee myself, — men-folks don't know much about cookin', ye see, — an' I let him have a hundred dollars just to start the thing. Wall, he brought the very fust one down to our house, 'n made a present on't to my wife; 'n, the minit she sot eyes on it, she took the sense o' the thing, and was sartin it wouldn't work. The idee was good enough for any thing *but* a warfle-iron; but ye couldn't make a warfle on it, to save your life. When the beak 'n the thunderbolts was done to a crips, the innards was 'most raw! Now that was Kernel Baker, — overdone in one spot, 'n underdone in another spot, 's long 's he lived.

"Wal, 's I was sayin', Marigold let him have two thousand dollars on his farm. The land ain't worth the money, you know, not even if you throw in the house and barn. But the kernel he had found a gold-mine up in the rocks on top o' the hill; 'n sure enough he did show some gold that he got out on't, 'n I guess that sort o' stirred old Marigold's blood. Ye know thet hole the kernel's cow fell into 'n' broke her neck? Wal, thet's the mine. They never could make it pay; 'n the kernel he pottered around about it, washin' an' 'malgamatin', 'an' the Lord knows what, till he got the rheumatiz, 'n salivated himself with the quicksilver, 'n kind o' run down an' died. Then Eliakim started off out West to seek his fortin'; an' Marigold promised him to wait five years, so's to give him a chance to redeem the old place. It w'an't wuth the money; but folks will get their hearts sot on the place they was born in, if it's too poor for a chicken-paster. Thet's nateral. But, afore the five years was up, Eliakim he'd took a fever out there in Illinois, 'n died, 'n left nothin'. So there was nobody but the widder 'n Jotham. I tell ye, Deacon it come mighty hard on Jotham to make up his mind to go away 'n leave his mother. He tried every way to git a livin' out o' the farm; but all he could do he couldn't more'n make both ends meet, 'n hard scratchin' at thet,— teachin' school in the winter, 'n workin' at Westcott's sawmill, besides all the farm-work 'n chores at home. Then come that courtin' business with Nancy; 'n Westcott didn't half like it. But the gal was headstrong, 'n there was nothin' to be said agin Jotham, only he was poor. But Westcott he had been poor himself, 'n he didn't stand so much on thet; only he said the young folks must wait. Fact is, Jotham was too proud to settle down onto a father-in-law, partic'ly with his mother. So he started off to sea. Advised him to go myself. He couldn't do so well any other way. It was a good chance,— supercargo I b'lieve they called it,— with middlin' fair pay, 'n the priv'lege o' speculatin' a little on his own hook. An' Lawyer Marigold he said he'd wait another year to see what'd come of it. I dunno how much you've heerd o' this afore, Deacon: what with Miss Peabody bein' so thick with Widder Baker, 'nd your Susan sech good friends with Jotham, it's more'n likely you kep' the run o' the whole thing. But what I'm comin' to'll be news to ye. About a week ago I see in 'The Advertiser' that Jotham's ship had been giv' up for lost, 'n the insurance company hed paid the insurance on her. That's a purty sartin sign, ye know. When one o' them companies pays up, it must be a tol'ble clear case.

"So, as I was sayin', I hitched up yesterday, 'n drove over to the Center, to see Lawyer Marigold about it. Says I, 'There's the Widow Baker without kith or kin, 'n how she'll git along 's more 'n I can see. Jotham left her his winter's 'arnin's; 'n the farm has jest about kep' her in vittles. One o' my men worked it on shares. But he give her all it perduced; 'n I made it all right with him. I wan't goin' to hev Jotham come back, 'n find we 'd let the old lady suffer. However,' says I, 'thet's no way to get along.'

"'Won't Westcott do nothin'?' says Marigold.

"'Westcott's not a bad man,' says I, 'if he *is* cluss. But I don't think the widow'd take any help from *him*. Ye see, she knows it was all along o' Nancy that her boy went off, 'n she takes it hard that Nancy hain't been to see her. Gals is gals, 'n I don't want to jedge 'em; but the fact is, Nancy never did care quite so much for Jotham as she made out to. 'N about a year arter he was gone, that smart young feller from Boston came a-cuttin round, 'n she was mightily taken with him. They say there wa'n't no reg'lar engagement between her an' Jotham: the old man wouldn't hear on't. So the long an' short on 't is, they're goin' to be married day before Christmas, 'n she's goin' to live in Boston, 'n keep her own kerridge. No wonder she was a little shy o' the widder!'"

The deacon listened to the squire's long story, and gently poked off with his whip the flies that settled on the white horse. His kind heart was beginning to stir within him, and to take an interest in the trials and sorrows of other people. "Seems to me," said the deacon, "I *hev'* heerd a good deal o' this afore; but I cal'late I've ben too much occupied with my own troubles. I sort o' let it go through my ears without stoppin'. I do remember Susan lettin' out the other day about Nancy Westcott, an' sayin' it was a shame she was goin' to git married; but I jest put it down as gals' talk. Wal, what did Lawyer Marigold say?"

"He said he hadn't no idee o' turnin' the Widow Baker out o' house 'an home at her age; but he didn't see no good o' leavin' on her there when she couldn't git her livin'. He guessed he'd hev to foreclose so 's to get a clear title to the farm, ef it ever should be worth any thing. Somebody'd hev to pay taxes, 'n' keep up the fences, an' so on. When the branch railroad come in to Hucklebury, the land might be wanted. It was a good place for a tunnel, anyhow. But he was ready to give a bond, that ef Widder Baker, or any other Baker, wanted the place back agin, they should have it for what it cost *him*.

"'Wal,' says I, 'Mr. Marigold, thet's fair 'n' square. As for the widder, I don't see but she'll hev to come on the town.'"

When Deacon Peabody heard that, he winced a little; but on second thought he said reflectively, "Wal, it ain't a disgrace, so far as I know, for a good woman to be took care of by her neighbors, when she's brought up her fam'ly well, 'n' lost 'em all, an' got beyond takin' care of herself."

"Jest so," replied the squire. "I thought I'd go over an' break it to her; but I didn't quite like to do it, partic'ly now, with this news about Jotham's ship bein' lost, an' the boy drowned. An' I had an idee that there wan't no need o' tellin' her the hull on't. We might auction off her board, accordin' to law; 'n' then the lowest bidder could jest step over, 'n invite her to stay with him."

The deacon suddenly broke off the conversation. "I must be gittin' on," said he, and addressed the white horse with a sudden "G'dap!" that surprised that venerable animal into a trot up hill. A listener unacquainted with the characters of these worthy people would have been shocked to hear a conversation which showed at least some faculty of sympathy and respect for the Widow Baker terminate with the cold-blooded proposition to put her up at auction as a pauper, and let her go to the citizen who would give her board and lodging for the smallest sum. Yet such a judgment would have been unjust. Under plain words and ways, both the squire and the deacon meant nothing but kindness. Either of them was ready to take the widow into his own home, and make her old age comfortable. Neither would have exacted payment from *her;* but that was no reason why the town shouldn't pay something for keeping her. Indeed, strange as it may appear, not only these two men, but many another substantial citizen, would have argued that whoever, not being a relative, and so bound to support her, should undertake her maintenance, ought, as a matter of right to his neighbors, to accept from the common treasury some payment for his pains. It was the only way in which all could contribute. This way of looking at the matter would not long have survived any considerable increase in the number of the poor. But Hucklebury had hardly any paupers. A blind man, a paralytic, and one or two old people who had, like Widow Baker, outlived their relations and means of subsistence, comprised the entire list. Every year the selectmen put them up at auction, after town-meeting; and on this small scale, and among such simple and kind-hearted folks, the plan worked well.

The deacon, softened by his own recent grief, and touched with the remembrance of the relations between his lost Cynthy and the Widow Baker, had made up his mind at once and irrevocably to give the latter a home in his own household. He didn't mean to wait for the auction even. He would take her in, if he had to pay her whole support himself. But, of course, he would bid, like other people; and no false delicacy would prevent him from accepting the stipend which the selectmen were bound to pay.

CHAPTER III.

BOARD AND LODGING.

WIDOW BAKER was in her sitting-room alone. It was not a handsome apartment: indeed, it had no element of beauty except that spotless neatness which is the sole adornment within the reach of poor folks. People used to say, "Widder Baker's settin'-room 's as clean 's a June sky," and the expression carried a sense of thoroughness with it which was well deserved. One was sure that under the clean rag-carpet there was an unstained floor, that the shining brass candlesticks on the mantelpiece hid no lurking windrows of dust, that under the settee, and behind the doors, and aways on the top-shelf of the dresser, a bride might have rubbed the finger of her white kid glove without sullying its purity. Just so unspotted of the world seemed Widow Baker herself as she sat in her high-backed rocking-chair, with her snowy cap, and her kerchief crossed on her breast, the great Bible open on her knee, and lying on its ample page her hands, clasped, and holding her silver-rimmed spectacles. It could not be a mere coincidence that the folded hands covered the words, "Though He slay me, yet will I trust in him."

The widow's eyes were turned to the wide prospect that spread itself beneath her windows; but she seemed to be looking far beyond over the blue horizon, beyond the valley fields, where the thick stubble told of the fruitful harvest; beyond the comfortable farm-houses, sending up banners of hospitality from their chimneys into the frosty air; beyond the fire-tipped steeple of the Hucklebury meeting-house; beyond the floating clouds and the crystal sky, — to " a better country, that is, an heavenly."

Deacon Peabody drove up to the gate, descended from his shay, hitched his horse (a superfluous proceeding), and walked into the house, shouting to the widow as he passed the window, " Don't ye git up now; jest set there comfortable, 'n' I'll open the door myself." But she arose, nevertheless, and met him at the threshold with a smile of grateful welcome.

" This is very good of you, Deacon," she said, " to think of me in your own sorrow."

" Yes," said the deacon, not meaning to accept the praise exactly, but following a habit of his, — " yes, I thought I'd come over 'n' see how ye was gittin' along. Putty cold spell yesterday 'n' to-day."

He looked at her as he spoke, with a sudden doubt whether she had heard the whole of the evil tidings concerning her own fate, — the loss of her last son, and the impending loss of home. Her placid air told him little; and it was to cover his embarrassment that he plunged into the subject, yet with an instinctive delicacy that the squire could never have imitated.

"We're right lonesome down to our house, Miss Baker, Susan 'n' me; 'n' it occurred to my mind that p'raps you'd be willin' to come down 'n' spend a — stay as long 's ye could, 'n' keep us company, Susan 'n' me. Susan misses her ma — 'n' so do I. You was a good friend to my Cynthy, 'n' I cal'late you'd be a good friend to her darter. 'S long's you expected to meet Jotham agin, it was nateral to want to keep a home for him. But" —

Here the deacon, remembering that perhaps she did not know of Jotham's death, hesitated for an instant, and then continued, "But ye know, if Jotham should come back, he'd be welcome too. Jotham's company is worth more'n his board any day."

"Phineas Peabody," said the widow earnestly, "you come like an answer to prayer! There's no news of my boy; and I should be wearied with waiting if I didn't know, that, wherever he is, he has not forgotten his mother. But I am sure he would not wish me to be a burden on my friends; and that I shall be, if I try to keep up the farm any longer. I'm too good a housekeeper, Deacon, not to have found out that the squire has helped a good deal this year. There's more oats and corn and potatoes than my half of the crops, and yet there'll be nothing to pay interest or debts. If Jotham comes back, he ought to start fair; and so — I've made up my mind — that the old place — will have to go. As for me — well, I've thought over it a good deal, and I'm not ashamed, in my old age, to be poor."

There were tears in her eyes, which the deacon did not see, because of something in his own. "Sho now; yes, yes," said the deacon hastily: "don't ye worry about that. You jest come 'n' visit with Susan 'n' me. That reminds me, I want you to kind o' doctor up Susan a little. There's suthin' the matter with her. She misses her ma, 'n' she don't have her uzhal appetite."

A few days after this conversation, the deacon's shay carried Widow Baker to her new home; and the deacon's lumber-wagon and ox-team followed with a load of bedding and furniture, — only one load, enough to furnish a single room. Close upon this event followed an auction of all the remaining personal property of the Baker family. The proceeds amounted to very little, — about two hundred dollars, — and the squire, somewhat to the surprise of the community, claimed the money in payment of his own advances during the past two years. It seemed to contradict his previous generous behavior; but the squire explained his conduct to the deacon in few words. "Two hundred dollars amounts to nothin'," said he; "but, 's long's the widder's got any money, we can't take her up 'n support her, accordin' to law. She'd hev to spend all her money fust. You jest give her a hint, Deacon: if she wants any spendin' money, she can draw on me, 'n' I'll make it right, besides, in my will." Moreover, it turned out that the squire had bought all the household stuff himself: so it was his own money he was saving for the widow.

Next came the auction of the farm under the foreclosure. That was bought by Lawyer Marigold, who, being able without cash expenditure to offer the full sum expressed in the mortgage, had no competitors. After the sale, however, there was a friendly and shrewd conversation between the lawyer and the deacon, which resulted in the absolute purchase of the farm by the latter for five hundred dollars.

Then came the queerest action of all, — the sale of the widow herself. This was not carried on with the noise and publicity of an ordinary public sale. The selectmen and freeholders simply talked the matter over, and the few paupers of Hucklebury were allotted to the lowest bidders for the privilege of boarding them. As for the Widow Baker, there was quite an animated competition for her. Plenty of people were willing to take her at small profit, and a few offered to accept the bare cost of her subsistence. But when the squire and the deacon began to bid below cost, "the boldest held their breath for a time." They ran down the scale with prudence, yet with firmness, until at last Phineas Peabody having bid two shillings a week — equivalent to thirty-three and one-third cents — the squire said, "Wal, Deacon, this is gittin' redic'lous. Ef ye don't look out, ye won't realize nothin' at all. But, sence you're bound to have the widder, I'll give up; 'n' I must say it's the best thing for both on ye."

All of which was quite unknown to the good old lady, who went on, in her quiet, cheerful resignation, "visiting" at the deacon's house. She did not know that the money which the deacon gave her every Sunday to put into the contribution-plate (aside from his own contribution, let us add) was the price of her board. But, if she had known it, her esteem for the deacon would not have been diminished; for she would have understood, as a stranger in Hucklebury could not have done, the combination of genuine kindness with habitual business-like exactness and economy which formed a part of the local character. In fact, the deacon was more delicate in his generosity than any of his neighbors would have been. It is true, not even they ever alluded to the widow's poverty in her presence; but that was chiefly because it did not occur to them as a matter separating them and her in any way. Their treatment of the poor, however disguised beneath the hard forms of a bargain, was in spirit more like the Christian communism of the New Testament than like the almsgiving of ancient (and modern) Pharisees.

But, as a bargain, the boarding of the Widow Baker was an unqualified success. It soon proved that she, and not her host, bestowed benefaction. What a blessing in the house is a serene and wise soul! What a contagious peace is that which is the fruit of sorrow rightly borne! The widow's unworldly spirit was not that of a dreamer. She was full of activity and helpfulness. She did not run from barn to kitchen, and from attic to cellar, like Susan; yet her directing mind was everywhere, and a new spirit of system and order began to pervade the establishment. The deceased Mrs. Cynthia Peabody had been one of those restless housekeepers who "fuss" when they are well, and worry when they are sick; and Susan, as the result of her tuition, was apt to bustle more, and plan less, than circumstances required. It was wonderful to see how, after the command of affairs had gradually lapsed into the old lady's hands, every thing began to work smoothly in doors and out. The very hired men on the farm caught the new fashion. The yard and the barn emulated the house in orderly neatness. The old white horse and the shay and harness were curried, washed, and oiled into new youth and beauty. The deacon's shirt-bosoms, and, what was more important, the deacon's brow, appeared without a crease or wrinkle. And, as a consequence of this universal decrease of friction, there was a saving of power in the whole machinery of house and farm. A shrewd observer like the deacon could not fail to see that the presence of this motherly guest was not only pleasant but profitable. And Squire Hawkins saw it too, and summed it up very neatly, when, in reply to old

Westcott's remark that "the deacon couldn't be makin' much, boardin' Granny Baker at two shillin' a week," he replied, "Wal, now, I dunno's Phineas Peabody kin make money so fast any other way as by boardin' Mis' Baker at two shillin' a week. I tell ye, Westcott, 'godliness is profitable;' 'n' the kind that Widder Baker has got is the quickest-payin' investment y' ever see."

This remark was made the week before Christmas, when Westcott was distributing invitations to his daughter's wedding with the gentleman from Boston. Hence the squire's concluding observation was not without point: "I won't undertake to say nothin' about young Jotham; but it's sartin' sure as you live, Westcott, your Nancy's missed the best mother-in-law that ever was raised in these parts. They don't hev 'em so good as that in Boston."

CHAPTER IV.

SUSAN PEABODY.

OF all who were blessed by the saintly and yet practical influence of the Widow Baker, Susan was, and had reason to be, the most grateful. She found what she had hitherto greatly lacked in two directions, — wise counsel in her daily duties on the one hand, and sympathy for all her aspirations on the other. It was Susan who first began to call the widow "Mother Baker;" and Phineas and the whole household followed her example. Indeed, it spread through the town; for she seemed like a mother to everybody.

No one ever heard her complain; and seldom did she speak of the sorrows of the past. But somehow, to Susan it was natural for her to talk about old times, and that led to the mention of later and later times, until at last all their conversations wound up with Jotham, as all roads lead to Rome. The difference between them was, that, while Mother Baker gradually settled into the conviction that her son was no longer on earth, and ranked him in her thoughts with the host of dear ones that waited for her in the new home that could not decay, nor be broken and scattered, Susan vehemently insisted that Jotham was still alive, and would return. "Two years is not so very long," she used to urge. "People are often missing for two years, — particularly in the East Indies."

And that creature, Nancy Westcott, had a letter from Jotham in her pocket, and never told anybody! It was rather embarrassing to her; and like a good many of us, when caught in the current of troublesome circumstances, she drifted in the vague hope that matters would somehow fix themselves. The chief elements of the case were these : first, she never had loved him " so very much as all that ; " secondly, his letter did not arrive until she had as good as accepted the Boston gentleman; thirdly, its contents were not satisfactory, as they told of shipwreck and disaster, and offered no other hope than that of further waiting until he could make a new start with "an idea" that he had, — for all the world just like his shiftless father; fourthly, of course he had written to his mother, and she knew all about it, and had probably informed him that Miss Westcott had thrown him overboard figuratively about the time that the typhoon had done him the same service literally; fifthly, why should she go to see his mother, just because he asked it, or write a letter to meet him on his arrival at Boston, which, of course, the Boston gentleman would not approve? sixthly, she would decide to-morrow or next day what to do about it; seventhly, she forgot all about it, except so far as an occasional momentary uneasiness might be called a recollection. So it came to pass that those who longed to see the living Jotham knew not of his coming, while she who knew it was not at all desirous of it. Once she might have told Susan as they met on the meeting-house steps; but Susan was "huffy," and carried her head very high, which made Miss Westcott huffy likewise: so they marched asunder, keeping their own secrets. "Heartless thing!" soliloquized Susan. "She's mad," thought Nancy, "because I'm engaged, and she ain't.

Shouldn't wonder if she stands up for Jotham Baker: she was always a friend o' his'n,—nothin' more'n a friend, though, that's one comfort. He's told me so a dozen times." Even after discarding her humbler lover, she didn't quite like to think of his "takin' up" with anybody else.

As for Susan, concealment was no "worm i' the bud" of her cheek. Since the coming of Mother Baker she had grown contented and even happy. She sang in the choir, and taught in the Sunday school, went to sewing-society and quiltings, patronized the very young gentlemen (who could be kept at a distance), made butter and pies, dried apples, preserved quinces, and attended to other duties daily and periodically, each in its season, as the almanac indicated, and with it all read poetry, and thought a good deal about Jotham,—in a sisterly manner, of course, and merely by way of indignation at the wrong that had been done him, and query whether he would feel it so much, when he should come home, as to go right away again in his despair. That would be very wrong, and she would certainly tell him so. It would be his duty to stay—on his mother's account.

A fortnight before Christmas came the cards which formally announced, what everybody knew, the ceremony of Miss Westcott's wedding. It was to be the sensation of the age for Hucklebury. Every thing was to be imported from Boston for the occasion, "down to the vittles and fiddlers." As Squire Hawkins said, adding, in his disenchanting way, " the settin'-room is goin' to be jest kivered with hemlock, 'n' I hev heerd that they intend to light up the stoop 'n' the .yard." Of course everybody was eager to be invited; and nobody was disappointed. Miss Westcott would not willingly omit a single witness to her triumph.

. Susan flung the cards into Mother Baker's lap, with a passionate exclamation of contempt. " To think ! " said she, " after the way she treated Jotham ! I won't go near her horrid wedding ! "

" My dear," said the placid old lady, with that innocent air which old ladies can assume when they are up to mischief, " you were a good friend to Jotham, and if he were alive " —

" He is alive ! I know he is," interrupted Susan.

" Well, do you want him to come home and marry Nancy Westcott against her will ? She was not bound to him, you know ; and she has found somebody who is better suited to her."

" How she could ever prefer that dandy to Jotham ! " said Susan hotly.

" *We* wouldn't, of course," replied Mother Baker. " But there's no accounting for tastes; and, if you stay away from her wedding on that account, won't folks say you think too much of — Jotham's mother ? "

This suggestion was sheer nonsense; but it had a startling effect upon Susan, who turned red and white in a moment, then blushed again to think that she had blushed, and at last said that she was sure there was something burning in the kitchen, whither she departed with all speed, and proceeded to quench the something that was burning by plunging her face into a basinful of cold water. The active preparations which began next day, in the way of clear-starching and ironing, indicated sufficiently that Susan was going to the party.

CHAPTER V.

JOTHAM.

In due course of time Mr. Jotham Baker, following pretty close upon his letter, landed in Boston, and, finding no news from home, made his way with all haste to his native town of Hucklebury. It was already dark when he arrived at the Center, where the stage stopped. Curiously enough he couldn't find a horse or a sleigh in the place. The tavern-keeper (a stranger to him) said they were all gone to Westcott's. Very well: the rest of the way, a good two-hours' walk, he would have to make on foot; but he stopped long enough to call at Lawyer Marigold's for the purpose of getting some news from home. The girl who came to the door did not recognize him, for two good reasons. In the first place, his full beard had changed his appearance: in the second place, she had never seen him, with or without a beard. So she told him merely that Mr. Marigold had gone to Westcott's, like everybody else, and shut the door in his face, with a promptness due to the coldness of the wintry air. The reply was a sort of omen to him; and, vaguely wondering why everybody had gone to Westcott's, he started off at a swinging pace over the crisp snow, bound for the same destination. That is, he started to go home; but the road would lead him past Westcott's.

Jotham, striding along the highway under the stars, was certainly a comely young fellow. Two years of adventure had made him stouter and browner, and for a shipwrecked wanderer he had a strange well-to-do appearance. People reduced to the extremity of poverty don't have such substantial baggage as the valise he had left in the Eagle Tavern, Hucklebury Center, nor wear such comfortable clothes as those in which he was now hastening homeward.

His thoughts, as he swiftly pursued his solitary way, were not altogether pleasant. First of all, he reproached himself for having left his mother alone two years before, and wondered whether Squire Hawkins had been, according to promise, a true friend to her. Jotham did not doubt that his mother knew of his return. To her he had written fully more than once. Why she had never received a single letter from him is one of the mysteries of the post-office, which, dear reader, the author is sorry to say nobody can clear up: hence it must be allowed to remain a mystery, as it is far too late now to ask for its investigation by a committee. Of all this Jotham was ignorant, but tormented himself, as he walked, with imagining what might have happened to his mother. Once he stopped suddenly — what if she were dead! Then he started again with violent speed, saying aloud, "No, no, *no!*" as if such a protest could affect the irrevocable past.

Then he thought of Nancy Westcott. What a strange thing it was, that, once out of her presence, he had found it so hard to believe in her sincerity! That letter which he had written to try her now seemed, on the whole, not a very honorable thing; though he had thought it fair at the time. Instead of telling her of his shipwreck, leaving her to infer that he was ruined, and asking her if she could wait for him a little longer, in the secret hope that she would not stand the test, he should have confessed frankly his own discovery that what he had thought love was only a transitory glamour.

"Jotham," said Jotham, "you are well paid for your shrewdness. You wanted to escape, and at the same time have the credit of being constant, though you pretended to *me* that it was your firm intention and desire to remain true to the girl if she was true to you. Now you've got to face the music. What if she is true to you? I shouldn't wonder if she was; it's as likely as not; it's very probable; by gracious, Jotham Baker, I believe it's so! Ugh, what a cold night!— and yet this walking makes a fellow perspire!

"And there's Susan Peabody, Jotham: what do you think of *her?* If you hadn't made a fool of yourself with Nancy, you might have had some chance, perhaps, with Susan. But she despised you after you went and gushed to her your silly nonsense about the other one. Don't you recollect when you told her? She never was the same to you after it came out who the girl was. No wonder: she was disappointed in you. *I* saw it, if *you* didn't. She had thought you had more sense. Don't flatter yourself she ever loved you, Jotham; she never dreamed of that: but she respected you until you made a fool of yourself. And you might have gone on from that to — O you donkey!"

He took a grim pleasure in this sarcastic soliloquy. But self-castigation soon tires both the executioner and the victim; and his muttered eloquence ended in a sigh as he approached the Westcott mansion, now glorious with streaming lights, and musical with voices and violins. The impulse of curiosity was too strong to be resisted, and, crossing the yard unnoticed, he gained a shadowed corner by one of the front-windows, whence he could survey the festive scene.

Almost the first person he distinguished from the

gay confusion was a dazzling being in white satin, with china-blue eyes, and flaxen locks erected into a stupendous structure above them, surrounded with a cloud of gauzy veil, and looking, on the whole, like a child substituted at the last moment for some larger bride, so that the wedding-dress should not be wasted. Only a second glance showed that the features were not merely childish. There was full-grown triumph in them, and a complete consciousness of the business aspects of matrimony. Jotham recognized at once the lady who would henceforward be known in New-England phrase as " she that was Nancy Westcott." The marriage was already over, and Miss Westcott was Mrs. — no, I won't give the name: I don't mean to pain anybody if I can help it; and the fact is, that the Boston gentleman some years after, having lost all his money by extravagance and speculation, signed another Boston gentleman's name to a check, and left the country. All the parties are dead long ago; but how do I know but they have relatives yet living, — relatives a great deal larger than I am?

In another instant Jotham saw Susan. Her dark hair and earnest eyes; her cheek, paler than when he had looked upon it last; her plain muslin dress, that showed so little fashion, and so much taste; every thing about her, in short, made her a complete contrast to the bride. To Jotham she seemed at once more beautiful and more unapproachable than ever before. There was a new expression on her face, which, of course, the foolish fellow could not read; the work of sorrow and patience bearing fruit of peace. All he felt was that she reminded him strangely of his mother, and that somehow, in spite of that, she was far beyond his reach. He could never talk with brotherly freedom to that dignified and lovely woman: he could only fall at her feet, and lie there till she left him in disdain.

As for the dandy in a white cravat, on whose arm "she that was Nancy Westcott" promenaded through the room, Jotham paid no attention to him; and why should we consider him? We always knew he would turn out badly, didn't we? To our hero he served as a slim piece of collateral evidence, corroborating the white satin and veil and orange-blossoms. Who he was didn't matter. He was *not* Jotham Baker — Hallelujah!

But man is ungrateful, and Jotham was not satisfied with his happy escape. He had made the important discovery that he didn't want Nancy because he did want Susan; and, being a young man of decision, he would not waste further time in useless repinings at the window. And he turned resolutely away to pursue his journey homeward.

But, as he passed the door, it was opened wide, and an imposing sable gentleman in white cotton gloves addressed him cordially with, "Second story front, sah!" This was one of the features imported for the occasion from Boston, — a darkey to open the door whenever he heard steps approaching. And our young man of decision, having determined to walk straight by, and being suddenly tempted by this dark and mysterious providence, was deflected ninety degrees from his course, and walked straight in.

Now, it happened that Nancy Westcott, just before coming down stairs to be married, had had occasion to rummage her bureau for a smelling-bottle, or a hair-pin, or something of that sort, and had suddenly come upon Jotham's letter, which, as a well-regulated person, she ought to have destroyed long before. There were too many women-folk fussing round to make it safe to destroy it now: so, with a hopeless glance at the fire, she thrust it into her dress, saying merely, — and that not for anybody's hearing, — "Goodness gracious!" Thus it came to pass that she was actually married with Jotham's letter in her bosom, — a horribly improper state of affairs!

During the solemn ceremony, which the parson made long enough to permit, if not to necessitate, some wandering of the thoughts, she perceived Susan Peabody, and made up her mind that Susan looked "stuck up," and didn't half realize the splendor of the occasion. Of course, if Susan was not suitably impressed, the admiration of all the rest would not suffice. That's human nature since the days of Haman. So, later in the evening, in fact, just at the moment when Jotham left the window, she got an opportunity to worry Susan, and began to do it with feminine skill.

"You haven't been introduced to my husband, Susan. You'd like him, I know. He says you're the most distangy woman in the room. But you an' me mustn't be rivals—*agin*. Hev you heard from Jo—from Mr. Baker lately?"

This was even more cruel than Nancy intended; for she really supposed the fact of Jotham's return was known to his friends, though she had never told of it, because she did not care to reveal her recent reception of his letter. It was much simpler to let her friends say, as they did, that there never had been any thing between him and her,—at least, nothing more than a flirtation.

But Susan was on her guard, and Nancy was no match for her. Without a sign of any emotion, not even scorn—she said slowly, "Mr. Baker has reason to congratulate himself."

That made Nancy "as mad as fire." She understood by it more than was meant; for it led her to suppose that Jotham, having been informed of her faithlessness, had pretended he was glad to be rid of her. Her breast heaved with passion, and fortunately (the bridal dress being a tight fit) that very heaving made her aware of Jotham's letter: otherwise there might have been a "scene." But this enabled her to restrain her wrath, and to say, in tones that attracted no attention from the rest of the company, "Perhaps he tries to make you think so, Miss Peabody. But that ain't the way he writes to me!" Whereat she pulled out the letter, thrust it into Susan's hand, and sailed away with her nose in the air, inwardly conscious that she had done a very foolish thing, and not at all aware that it was the best thing that could have been done for everybody but herself.

Susan recognized the handwriting; seized the letter; forgot Nancy, the company, every thing; made her escape blindly out of the room; and rushed upstairs to the ladies' dressing-room (second story back), clasping the letter in her hand. Jotham was alive!

Nobody was in the room. She could read the letter unobserved. In her tumultuous happiness she was about to kiss it; but her eye fell on the address, — "Miss Nancy Westcott" (she had forgotten for a moment to whom the letter had been written). As for kissing "Miss Nancy Westcott" — that was a little too much. But she did open the paper, and put to her lips a carefully-selected spot on the inside, which bore the words, "Yours truly, Jotham Baker." Then she hastily read the letter; and not even its apparent testimony that he still loved the heartless creature down stairs could silence in her heart the singing voice, "Jotham is alive!"

Meanwhile the young man himself had left the window, walked slowly, though decidedly (as I have before mentioned), to the front-door and into the hall, and was at this moment at the top of the stairs, on his way to the second story front; so that, when Susan raised her eyes from the perusal of his letter, she saw him passing the door.

With a cry of joy she sprang forward, calling his name; but, as he turned, she recollected what must be his present anguish, and said only, holding out both hands, "O Jotham, I'm so sorry for you!"

Alas! what a comedy of errors it was! Poor Jotham, already in a maze of conflicting emotions, lost his head entirely at hearing her friendly words, and burst into an incoherent explanation about Nancy and his own affections, out of which confusion emerged presently a declaration of love to Susan. This he made still worse by dropping on his knees before her, as he had just been wildly dreaming he would do some day. He was a handsome fellow; but no fellow ought to kneel down in his overcoat. He deserved to be laughed at for his pains. But Susan was in no mood for laughing. Her maidenly pride burned hotly in cheek and eye. "Mr. Baker," she said with bitter politeness, "now you're down, perhaps you will have the goodness to pick up that letter. Nancy gave it to me, and I will take this opportunity to return it to the writer."

She watched him with unmoving look as he clutched the letter, recognized it, rose, and staggered from the room. Down stairs he rushed, and past the astounded doorkeeper, into the open air. She listened until she heard the bang with which the door closed behind him; then, having nothing else in the world to do, Susan Peabody fainted away, and fell on the spot where he had knelt.

CHAPTER VI.

HOW THE WIDOW INTERFERED.

JOTHAM felt, as he reached the road, as if he had escaped from a burning house in which was every thing he held dear in life. But his second thought was of his mother. He had her to live for, at least; and to her he would devote himself. So he hastened up the hill-road, past the squire's farm, and on to the well-remembered house where he expected to find her. It was always a rather lonesome place; but to-night, as he approached it, and saw neither light in the windows, nor living thing about the yard, a chill struck his heart. The barking of a dog, or the deliberate rising of a cow disturbed in her repose by his passage, would have been most welcome. His knocking at the door called forth no answer; and when, after fruitless shouting, he lifted a window-sash, climbed into the sitting-room, struck a light, and found the place dismantled and empty, — except for that "litter" peculiar to an abandoned room, which told him more plainly than any thing else that his neat and efficient mother could no longer be in authority there, — the revulsion was overpowering. The stalwart young fellow dropped his match, and, leaning in the darkness against the mantel-piece, cried as if his heart would break. This blow was indeed the worst of all.

A moment later he was again out of doors, and rushing down the hill-road at a terrible pace. As he passed the lane that turned down to the squire's house, a sleigh came up with much clangor of silvery bells, bringing the squire and Mrs. Hawkins, who were just returning from the party at Westcott's.

"Jerusalem!" ejaculated the hearty squire, "ef that ain't Jotham! Whoa, there! Why, Jotham, how d'ye do? Where did ye come from? 'n' how on airth — but here! git right in, there's room for ye; come right along to the house."

"The house is empty," said Jotham in quick, hoarse tones. "What has happened? Where's my mother?"

"She's boardin' at Deacon Peabody's," replied the squire; "'n' she looks twenty years younger for't. You jest come along. Ye can't see your mother to-night; 'n' ye mustn't see her nohow, till I've put ye up to the news."

So Jotham spent the rest of a long evening and the night at the Hawkins's, and slept soundly in spite of his sorrows. The squire told him all about every thing, dwelling particularly on Susan and her affection for his mother, and much surprised that Jotham regarded that subject with evident pain.

"What's the matter with ye, Jotham?" pursued the squire. "Now, I'm a plain man, 'n' I go to the pint. It ain't no use for you to worry about Nancy Westcott—though she'd be a pretty good match, jest now, for a feller as poor's you be."

"I don't care a sixpence for Nancy Westcott," interrupted Jotham sullenly, "and I'm not so poor as you think."

"Why, the hull cargo was lost, I cal'late: them companies wouldn't 'a' paid the insurance without proof o' that "

"Exactly. *They paid the insurance*, and my goods were insured, as well as the rest. I knew that would be all right, and I bought a home cargo on the strength of it, and made enough by the voyage to give me a good start."

"Ginger an' spices *has* riz," said the squire thoughtfully. "I read that in 'The Advertiser' last week. Dew tell! Wal, Jotham, I'm glad on't. But don't ye go to buyin' back the old farm: it'll ruin ye, sure."

"On the contrary," said Jotham, "I shall buy it at once, and sell the mine-hill to a man who is coming up from Boston right away to look at it."

"What!" cried the squire, "gold, arter all?"

"No; granite."

"Wal, there's plenty o' that on't," said the squire.

"Yes; and it will be the best place for a quarry that can be found when the branch railroad is built. But I don't care much about it now, except for mother's sake," added Jotham with a sigh.

The squire looked at him shrewdly. "My boy,"

said he, "there's somethin' the matter between you an' Susan, 'n ye'd better tell me all about it. I ain't one that'll talk about it, like the women-folks." (Mrs. Hawkins had retired, or this remark would have been suppressed.)

Jotham made a clean breast on this invitation, first handing over the unlucky letter as a text, and then furnishing a full commentary upon it. At the conclusion, the squire whistled reflectively, and at last delivered his opinion: —

"It looks like a bad job, Jotham; but I've seen wuss. Susan was glad to see ye — stick a pin there! An' she was mad to hev ye make a fool o' yourself, 'n' try to made a fool o' her. Wal, now, look at it cool an' reasonable, 'n' who wouldn't be? I tell ye what," continued the squire, warming up as he went on, "it's all right, an' so you'll see. You go to bed!"

Meanwhile Susan, whom we left "all in a heap" on the floor of the "second story back," had recovered from her faint without help, and without attracting attention. Of course her first act was to scrub and rub her pale cheeks till they glowed, replace and tighten various hair-pins (which always become loose in moments of emotion), and obliterate the traces of her agitation. Then she went down stairs, found her father, and persuaded him to take her home, — no difficult matter, since he was bored with the newfangled stiffness of the entertainment. On the way they spoke little. Phineas was occupied with driving, and only once put a question to his daughter: —

"Hope ye had an interestin' time, Susan?"

"Yes, very interesting," said she, and lapsed again into silence. But her thoughts were busy enough, recalling painfully the strange behavior and incoherent speech of Jotham, and wondering whether she had not done him some injustice. That letter of his to Nancy was not so very loving. There was a mystery in it; and an old friend should not be discarded without an opportunity to explain his conduct. Perhaps he was at this moment with his mother. He was an affectionate and dutiful son, at least. "Couldn't you drive a little faster, father?" said Susan.

But on arrival she found that Mother Baker was in bed, and that nobody had called. She kept the secret of Jotham's return. Why should she say any thing to her father about it? Everybody would know it in the morning. But, when the morning came, she was thoughtful enough to prepare the widow for the joyful surprise of meeting her son, assuring her that he had really returned, and would soon make his appearance, but declining to tell how she had got the news, except that she had heard it at the party.

When Jotham knocked at the door, it was Susan, much to his embarrassment, who opened it. He began an apology for his intrusion, which she checked with a gesture. "Your mother is expecting you," said she, pointing to the door of the room in which the widow was sitting, and withdrew, to fidget in the kitchen; while Jotham, forgetting for the moment all woes and embarrassment, entered to clasp in arms of unalterable affection and perfect joy the darlingest old mother that ever lived. .

Widow Baker was so glad to get her son back on any terms, that she needed little to satisfy her curiosity concerning his long absence and silence. When he alluded to letters he had written her, she did not tell him, in this first happy hour, that she had never received them. When he mentioned to her his plan about the old place, which he had already found he could buy back, and which would be, after all, a source of profit to the family, her face lit up with a proud smile such as the late Colonel Baker might well have returned to enjoy. "That's what your father always said," was her comment. Dear soul! she had put sympathy, if not faith, in every one of her husband's schemes ; and it was to her simple affection a sort of vindication of his misunderstood and depreciated career, to have his gold-mine turn out at least a granite-quarry.

"Well, my son," said the widow at last, "the deacon'll be glad to have you stop here for a while, until you can set up a house of your own. He told me that when he first invited me. I wouldn't have come to a house, you know, where my boy would not have been welcome." This was the good lady's artful approach to a subject that lay near her heart.

"The deacon is a true friend," replied Jotham, "and I shall tell him so. But I — I'd rather not stop in his house. Don't you think you could visit somewhere else, — say, at Squire Hawkins's?"

"Why, what should I do without Susan?" was the deeply innocent reply; to which Jotham made a somewhat testy rejoinder:—

"You'll have to do without Susan sooner or later, and you might as well begin!"

Now, by this time, Susan, having rattled about the kitchen vigorously, doing nothing, for half an hour, had found it absolutely necessary to come to the sitting-room. She wanted a "holder" to protect her fair fingers in lifting a kettle from the fire; and the holder in the kitchen didn't suit her — no, not at all. But there was one in the sitting-room that would suit, and that one she must have. So, with a timid preliminary knock on the half-open door, she walked in. The widow watched her keenly.

"Susan," she said, "our Jotham has come!"

"Yes," replied Susan, with a beating heart, and a voice far too unsteady for the leading soprano of the Hucklebury choir, "I've met Mr. Baker already. I — I hope he's very well." Upon this she went towards the fireplace, where the "holder" hung on a nail, and, before she got there, forgot what she was going for, and so, coming to a dead stop, looked into the fire with preposterous earnestness and a great desire to cry. Jotham, on his part, studied a spot on the floor till it began to revolve before his eyes in an amazing way, and then said hastily that he thought he had better go and attend to some other matters.

"Don't go on my account," said the young girl at the fire; at which Jotham stopped short, and the situation was worse than ever. But the widow, bless her! was more than equal to it. She divined the state of affairs better than if they had told her all about it, though that's not saying much; for, if they had undertaken to tell her, a pretty mess they would have made of it with their confusions and cross-purposes and reservations and pique and embarrassments.

"I want Jotham to visit with us a few days, till he gets ready a place of his own,— for him and me," said she; "but he thinks he had better not."

"I suppose he is right," remarked Miss Peabody to the fire."

"He wants me to go and stay somewhere else with him," continued the widow.

Susan turned half round, with a sudden movement, and then resolutely back to her former position, saying earnestly,—

"No, no! you mustn't leave us. Nobody can do without you, dear Mother Baker!"

It was strange that she could not even face her dearest friend, wasn't it? But the fact is, she had come in a hurry, and her handkerchief was missing, as handkerchiefs are so apt to be at the very minute when they are worth their weight in gold.

"If anybody needs me, then my only son needs me most," said the old lady, going over to Jotham, and putting her thin hands on his broad shoulder. "Where he had better not stay, I will not stay."

"Then he must stay," said the voice by the fire. "He needn't go on my account."

"Mother," interrupted the subject of this dialogue, shaking off his wretched timidity, and speaking in a straightforward, commanding way, that settled things at once in his favor (though he was not aware of that), "don't trouble Miss Peabody any further. She has reason to think I have treated her with some indignity, though she is wrong: I would die first."

"Of course," said the widow heartily. "But Susan don't believe any such thing. Why, she can't: it's impossible. — O Susan! shake hands with Jotham, and tell him so yourself."

Susan held out her hand with averted face; but the young man was bent on no half-way measures. "No," he said imperatively. "Hear me out. She is wrong in her thought of me, though I am to blame for her mistake; but she is right in saying (as she did before you spoke of leaving here) that I had better not stay in this house."

Miss Peabody had withdrawn again her neglected hand, and, having no better use for it, was pressing it against her heart, — a most insipid and unprofitable use of both hand and heart. Mr. Jotham Baker, having the floor, went on, as is the custom of orators, addressing the chair, but meaning to be heard by the audience : —

"For I love her — I love her dearly; and I will not stay in her house, or touch her hand, or look into her face — because I couldn't bear it. I don't want to be 'old friends' again."

"You'd better stay," said Susan feebly. "Your mother wants you to stay."

The Widow Baker smiled, as a general might smile, who, just as he was about to order a retreat, should see through his field-glass the white flag hoisted by the enemy. But Jotham had no field-glass, and went on with his last despairing volley.

"No," he said impatiently, "it is impossible. If — if you felt as I do, you would understand me. But I do not deserve to be utterly despised; and I think, Miss Peabody, that I ought to explain to you before I go "—

Susan shook her shoulders. "I don't want any explanation," she said.

"And *I do*," said desperate Jotham. "I claim it as a right: it is my last chance, and I *will* be heard."

That obstinate young woman put her fingers in her ears, and that obstinate young man went right on addressing the chair; and the chair, that is to say, Widow Baker, positively laughed in his face. The sublime was evidently sliding fast — *facilis descensus* — into the ridiculous.

Now, this scene would not have lasted half as long if Susan had had a handkerchief. When a person has been crying ever so little, and is obliged by circumstances to dry before the fire, without the aid of cambric or bandanna, the conversation must be prolonged, to give that person a reasonable time. But if the person begins again — why, then all subterfuges are in vain. Thus it came to pass that Susan, whose fingers were not so very tightly pressed into her ears, heard Jotham walk towards the door. The blundering, lucky fellow! Just as he was about to resign the game, he gave checkmate. For Susan Peabody turned like a flash, and called him by name — no mistake about it, and no "Mr." — a good, clear, unfaltering "Jotham!"

But he was smitten with blindness. Not even the sight of her, blushing, tearful, radiant, holding out both hands towards him, could make him understand.

"Then you will hear my explanation?" said stupid Jotham.

"I tell you," said she, stamping with her little foot, "I have heard enough, I won't have any explanations!"

"But before I go" — pursued the incorrigible Jotham.

"Mr. — Jotham — Baker," said Susan, laying down the proposition with the air of a teacher whose patience was exhausted, and emphasizing it with a didactic forefinger, "your mother — and I — are — never — going — to — let — you — go — away — from us — as — long — as — you — live: *so, there!*"

Here the Widow Baker, who had so wisely interfered, perceived with equal wisdom that her interference was no longer called for. And her departure from the room cuts short my story at this most interesting point; for, although I am very intimate with all the parties, Susan and Jotham never would repeat to me — and I am utterly unable to imagine — the conversation that followed.

SKETCHES OF WESTERN TRAVEL.

WONDERS OF THE YELLOWSTONE.

I.

AN EXPLORING PARTY.

LAST summer[1] two of us found ourselves, on professional duty connected with "the development of the mineral resources" of our country, in the Territory of Montana, to wit, the capital thereof, Virginia City; and there we did devise a journey up the Madison Valley to the Spouting Geysers, over the mountains to the lake, cañon, cataracts, and hot-springs of the Yellowstone, and so on, as events might determine; traversing, in short, that large area of nearly four thousand square miles, of which Congress has wisely made a National Park. Our party was not a full-fledged affair, with wings of military escort, and claws of tools and instruments for detailed scientific investigation, but an assemblage of volunteers, comprising no small amount of original and unconventional character.

[1] The summer of 1871.

Numerous eminent citizens of Virginia City had enthusiastically declared their intention of joining our company, and we reasonably expected to invade the mountain solitudes with a great array of rank and intellect. But, when the critical day arrived, there was an amazing pressure of business, legal and otherwise, in the usually somewhat dull town, which hindered every one of our distinguished friends from starting. Far be it from me to suggest that a very recent raid of the Sioux into the Gallatin Valley had any thing to do with this unanimous inability to go where glory waited. That could not be; for did not each reluctantly declining friend take pains to add, "There'll be no danger, I guess, where you are going. You just keep a good lookout, and you'll get through all right, I guess. Got plenty of arms and ammunition, haven't you?"

Under these inspiring encouragements we prepared to set forth. There were six of us men, eight of us horses, and one of us mule. Gilman Sawtelle, the guide, will forgive me for bringing him before the public by name. I can not rank him with any of the typical pioneers, from Leatherstocking down, who have been familiar in novels of Western life. He affects no singularity of dress or speech; indulges not in long and silent laughter; prefers not an old single-barreled, small-bore, muzzle-loading Kentucky rifle to the modern arms of precision; does not pretend to see in the night as well as in the daytime, or to follow a trail where there isn't any; misses a shot now and then, at long range, like any other honest man; reads books and newspapers; and does not despise his kind. A stalwart, blond, blue-eyed, jovial woodsman is he, who for years has kept a solitary ranch on the bank of Henry's Lake, some sixty miles from the settlements. Half a dozen well-built log-houses constitute his establishment. There is a comfortable dwelling, a stable, a work-shop, store-houses for skins and game, and an ice-house. Mr. Sawtelle's principal business has been spearing trout, packing them in ice, hauling them in wagons to Virginia City, and even as far as Helena, and disposing of them at handsome prices to the busy population who haven't time to fish for themselves. A farm supplies him with vegetables and grain; the valleys afford him excellent hay; and land and water all about him swarm with game of every kind.

Mr. Thrasher the photographer is another character of public interest, whom I will not disguise under a fictitious name, because the one he wears by right exactly suits him. He invests the profession of photography with all the romance of adventure. What other men will do for self-defense, or excitement, or a positive reward, he does for a "negative." No mountain is too high for him, if there's a "view" from the top. No perilous precipice daunts him, if it is just the place for his camera. If there is a picturesque region where nobody has been, thither he hastens, with company if company offers; alone if need be, he and his pack-mule, carrying the precious chemicals and glasses. Sometimes, after a long and arduous expedition, that mule will roll down a steep mountain-face, and smash every thing. Then Thrasher begins again, nothing daunted. It is a sight to see him, when, struck by the beauty of some sudden vista, he halts, and rapidly unpacks, erecting his tripod, and hanging to the bough of some convenient tree his black-cloth laboratory. In a trice the plate is prepared, the view is taken: Thrasher buries his head, ostrich-like, in the dark chamber, exposing recklessly, as he kneels at his work, the dilapidated rear of his corduroys. Then speedily comes from the black tent a muffled shout of triumph, and the artist emerges backward on all-threes, holding up a dripping negative for general admiration. Or perhaps it doesn't suit him, and the boys are told to go on; he will stay and "wrastle" with that view; and an hour after camp is made, when all have subsided into the delights of *dolce far niente*, — supper being over, and guard not begun, — along comes Thrasher with "that cussed mule," who will persist in trying to carry her unwieldy pack between precisely the trees that stand too close for passage, — Thrasher, I say, weary, hungry, irate, but victorious.

I may mention here, that, after we had been several weeks in the mountains, Mr. Thrasher became entirely unmanageable. He had so many views to take that there was no hope of getting him back to civilization until his chemicals were used up — and he had provided a desperately large stock. So on the cañon of the Yellowstone we left him, with Sawtelle; while the rest of us rode home without him. I have heard since that he got "burnt out" by a forest fire, losing every thing *but his negatives;* and that after returning to Virginia City, and procuring a new outfit, he posted back again, this time alone, to "do the rest of that country, or bust."

O Thrasher! Thy mule, with the sharp-pointed legs of the camera-tripod projecting from her stern, was unpleasant to the next-following horseman when she backed in a narrow defile; nor was it altogether delightful to get up prematurely in order to form part of one of thy frequent "sunrise scenes:" but thou wert most excellent company on the march and in camp, and thy energy and enthusiasm were sublime. May I not fail to fare with thee again, some day, through wild and rugged ways, pursuing with tireless steps the spirit of beauty to her remotest hiding-place!

Another member of the party was Mr. Hardpan, of the editorial staff of "The Weekly Alloutdoors," published at Bucksborough, Montana, — a fine specimen of the frontier "local," possessing the wide-awake characteristics of the city species, but superior in point of manliness. Interviewing people against their will, following with intent nose the trails of scandal, picking up scraps of information around the doors of public offices, and the like occupations, tend to obliterate in the city reporter somewhat of the gentleman, and more of the man. But the habit of traversing mountains and valleys in search of news, interviewing the hardy miners and hunters in the gulches or by the camp-fire, "prospecting" *en route* for wash-gold or quartz (for your Western editor has always been at some time a miner himself, and can not pass black sand or rusty rock without "just taking a look at her"), not disdaining to follow the fleet deer, and impale the wrigglesome trout, nor shirking the due share of danger before the grizzly or the Sioux, — this life, I say, makes quite another man of the reporter. Paul Pry and Hardpan have nothing in common: in fact, one would not have imagined that the gentleman from "The Weekly Alloutdoors" was an emissary of the press at all. If he "took notes," it was in secret, as a gentleman should. He has since immortalized us all in a highly embellished account of the journey; but he inflicted upon us no preliminary tortures during the trip, and the picture he has painted is as delicately and truthfully flattering as one of Huntington's portraits, or Sarony's photographs. It is a comfort to "sit" to an artist who will see to it that freckles are omitted, and that a pleasing expression is secured at any cost. For the rest, Hardpan was a

jolly companion, who obtruded no "shop-talk," and
endeared himself to all by his extraordinary skill in
the preparation of "dough-gods" and "bull-whacker's
butter,"— two triumphs of camp-*cuisine* not to be
compassed by any thing short of genius.

The other three of us decline to be publicly por-
trayed; but we permit it to be said, in all modera-
tion, that we possessed among us all the beauties
of form and feature, all the virtues of character, and
all the varieties of learning and accomplishment,
that anybody ever found in anybody. What one
of us lacked another was sure to have — until that
woeful day when none of us possessed so much as a
pipeful of "Lone Jack;" but this deficiency was
abundantly remedied as soon as we returned to the
settlements, and we now present to the pen of the
eulogist our pristine perfection.

But how can we omit to mention Sawtelle's dog? —
ugliest, hardiest, most enthusiastic and affectionate,
most ardent in the chase, most patient in hunger,
and insensible to fatigue, of all the canine race, — a
dog of no distinguished lineage, and no advantage
in early education, but full of an excellent spirit
and a companionable soul. The enthusiasm with
which that dog would attempt the impossible, —
chasing grouse upon the wing, or swimming fiercely
after ducks that contemptuously waited for him till
he almost touched them, and then, just as he raised
his yelp of anticipated triumph, dove under him, and

re-appeared behind him, to his blank bewilderment,—the brisk enthusiasm with which he would essay these feats, stimulated every day by the remembrance of past failures to wilder racing and louder yelping, was a moral to mortals. Some day, I am persuaded, that dog *will* catch a grouse upon the wing, or a duck upon the wave. Nothing can be impossible forever to such perseverance. He rejoiced in several names, being chiefly called Bob, for short, in allusion to his tail.

With the remainder of our party, that is to say, with the horses and the mule, we began to get acquainted very early in the journey. The first day's march was a succession of packings, chasings, shoutings, draggings, and buckings, from the time we were escorted out of Virginia City by the merchant-princes, legal luminaries, and small boys of the town, until we made camp on the other side of the "divide," after dark, cold and hungry and tired, by the rushing waters of the Madison. It took some time, however, to learn all the peculiarities of all the animals, and to produce in them the sure conviction that we knew their tricks and their manners. One ancient white steed, who was used to carrying packs, infected the rest with his wisdom. He taught them to swell up when they were "sinched," so that the girths might slip afterward; to lie down and roll with their packs on; to start on wild prairie gallops without warning, and work their burdens around their bellies, where they could be conveniently kicked; to "buck," when they could thereby throw any body or any thing into a river; and at night, when they were turned out for rest and grazing, to start in solemn procession for home, and travel a dozen miles before daylight. But that sublime being, man, is more than a match for that noble animal, horse; and due subordination was ere long established. Did time permit, I would gladly sing the praises of the "diamond hitch," — that mystery of ropes and running-knots, which, once properly adjusted upon a well-balanced and well-settled load, defies the cunning of the equine or asinine bearer, and will not even yield to a pine-tree, tearing and scraping against it in the forest. But we have lingered too long already over the incidentals of our trip — though, in truth, they are rather to be reckoned as essentials; for the destination of a journey like ours may be wherever you please, if you are well fitted out for the march and the camp; but without good company, good arms, and a knowledge of the "diamond hitch," one had better not start at all.

II.

UP THE MADISON.

As I have hinted, our party was escorted out of Virginia City by the friendly population, and took its way over the divide which separates that town from the valley of the Madison. And here, O unsuspecting reader! shall be sprung upon thee a trap of instruction. But be not dismayed, the agony shall be brief. And, moreover, there is no dread examination awaiting you beyond, to reveal your wicked neglect if you skip the next paragraph altogether. Geography is not pleasant, but grievous; yet is it necessary to him who would travel, whether in person or by sympathetic imagination. Wherefore listen: —

The two great river-systems of the Missouri-Mississippi, on the one hand, and the Snake-Columbia, on the other, have their highest sources close together, in the Rocky Mountains, where their upper waters even pass each other in opposite directions, like the fingers of two hands, employed in the fascinating game of

> "Here's the church, and here's the steeple:
> Open the door, and there's the people!"

Persons who do not know this game will be bewildered by the illustration, just as persons who enter for the first time the country of which I speak are bewildered when they find one stream running north for the Gulf of Mexico, and the next running south for the Pacific Ocean. For this perplexity, dear reader, there are only two remedies: you must either learn the game, or visit the region.

It is the Missouri system which chiefly concerns us here; and it must suffice to say of it that four large rivers rise not far from the north-west corner of Wyoming Territory, and flow for some distance northward. Three of them — the Jefferson, the Madison, and the Gallatin — unite at Gallatin City, Montana, to form the Missouri, which continues northward to near the British boundary, which it avoids by a great bend to the east, after which it gradually assumes a southeast course to the Mississippi. The fourth river is the Yellowstone, which bends on its own hook, so to speak, before reaching the Missouri, and finally joins that river on the borders of Dakota. In the upper part of their course, therefore, the valleys of the Jefferson, Madison, Gallatin, and Yellowstone, are in a general way, parallel, and their order from west to east is indicated by the order in which I have named them. The Gallatin, being the shortest, rises farther north than the others, and the headwaters of the Madison are separated from the Yellowstone Lake, which may be called the head of the

Yellowstone, by mountain-ranges only. To traverse, mainly by valley routes, the geysers of the Upper Madison (or Fire Hole River), the Yellowstone Lake, cañon and cataracts, and the hot-springs that dot the region between these rivers, one may either ascend the Yellowstone, cross the mountains to the Madison, and descend the Madison, or *vice versa*. The first is what the parties of Washburne and Hayden did. The second is what our party did — only we left the Yellowstone after following it down to the great cañon, and returned by a different trail across the mountains to the Madison Valley, by which we returned to the settlements. Here endeth the first lesson in geography.

Sawtelle and his dog did not share in the triumphal departure from Virginia City, but awaited us at the camp on the Madison, nine miles from town. Next morning, being the 10th of August, we began our journey in earnest, and traveled eighteen miles up the valley, — a fair day's work for the pack-animals, though on our way home we "pushed things" over the same ground at the rate of thirty miles daily. The valley of the Madison at this point is an inspiring scene. The river is accompanied on the east by the splendid chain of the Madison Mountains, with their bold outlines, rugged brown-and-red rock-surfaces, snow-touched crests, and occasional tracery of piney cañons. Opposite these is a succession of inferior but picturesque ridges, and between is the broad, fair, grassy valley, — a very paradise for stock-raisers. To the north, it draws together into the dark and precipitous lower cañon of the Madison. Southward (i.e., up the valley), the benched or terraced structure of the terrain becomes more and more distinct, until at last three or four gigantic terraces, rising one above another from the stream to the mountains, stretch away for many miles on either side along the valley. What a natural preparation for a railroad! The engineer need only choose his level, and then "go it" on a gravel foundation hundreds of feet deep. There is more or less volcanic rock all along the ranges; but as we ascend the river it becomes predominant, and forms at length high lava-walls, like the Palisades of the Hudson. Upon these lavas and the gravel terraces, the vegetation is scanty, though the clear mountain-streams which cut their way through deep side-cañons at intervals of about ten miles are delightfully shadowed with pines and cottonwoods and fringed with verdure. The general aspect of the scenery, after the meadows are left behind, is desolate and grand.

Impossible to describe is the quiet beauty of an evening or noon-day camp by a rushing stream in these sublime solitudes, — the blazing fire, the luxurious repose of man and beast, the fragrant pipe, well chosen by some early poet of coppery hue as *par excellence* the emblem of peace! Grouse strut and flutter in the bushes; eagles scream and wheel in the sky; processions of ducks make straight, swift course down the river; the service-berry thickets and the freshly-turned stones and stumps betray the recent presence of the fruit and insect loving bear (no bug-bear to us and our repeating breech-loaders); there are upon the trail delicate footprints of antelope and deer, and heavy hoof-marks of the elk. From our green, cool covert we look lazily out upon the valley, hot with the meridian glow, or vast and hazy in the twilight, or mystical and solemn beneath the moon.

On the fourth day we reached the middle cañon of the Madison, where the river breaks through the main chain of the Rocky Mountains; and, to avoid the difficulty of the passage, we turned out of the valley, crossed the low divide known as the Reynolds Pass, and saw before us the gleaming waters of Henry's Lake. Here we found hospitable shelter in Sawtelle's ranch, and excellent amusement for a day in hunting and fishing upon his preserves. What with innumerable grouse on the hillsides, ducks and geese in the sedgy sloughs, snowy swans and pelicans upon the lake, and four-footed game of every variety in forest and field, the sportsman's taste can not fail to be gratified. If he is an adventurous Englishman, and must have danger, let him hunt skunks: there are plenty of them, and they strike fear into the stoutest heart.

Who was Henry? and how came he to have a

lake? Henry was a prominent fur-trading capitalist of early days, I believe, and had this geographical greatness thrust upon him. Henry's Lake is the source of the Henry, or north fork of the Snake. It is surrounded by lofty mountains, but connected with the outer world by four remarkably low passes, all practicable, and two of them (Snake River and the Reynolds Pass) positively inviting, for a railroad. Southward, the north fork runs with steady grade out to the great plains of Idaho. North-west, a pass over a low divide leads to Red Rock Lake, the head of a branch of the Beaverhead and the Jefferson. Northward, the Reynolds Pass communicates with the terraced valley of the Madison; and eastward, the Henry Pass gives easy entrance to the great Madison basin, above the middle cañon. Here endeth the second lesson in geography,

Our route lay through the latter opening; and a charming day's ride it was, from the placid lake, through the glens and glades of the pass, beneath the shining summits, along the willowy banks of the streams, by the great beaver-dams, and finally across the wide basin, densely covered with slender pines, until we camped again on the banks of the river we had left two or three days before.

At this camp we got a taste of the mosquitoes and black flies, which taught us that the country did not swarm with game exclusively for us. After a fellow has been slaughtering the inhabitants of the wilderness for a week, it is, perhaps, a wholesome lesson for him to be slaughtered in turn. The helplessness of man against insects is one of Nature's sarcastic comments upon intellect. Camels we can manage, swallow even, if necessary; but gnats are too many for us. Our unfortunate animals couldn't eat, but wound themselves up in their lariats, in frantic attempts to get away from the multitudinous foe. Old Whitey showed his sagacity by quietly usurping the smoky side of the camp-fire, whence he was not to be enticed away. An hour after sunset, however, the cold stiffened all winged nuisances,— an August night in these latitudes means frost,— and, before they thawed out in the morning, we had sounded our "packs, saddles, and away!"

III.

MARCH AND CAMP.

The great Madison basin is perhaps thirty miles wide by fifty long. The river enters it on the south by a narrow cañon, which now lay before us, and leaves it on the north by the cañon we had avoided in our *détour* by Henry's Lake. The southern cañon, upon which we entered after crossing the basin, is nine or ten miles long, and extremely picturesque. Basaltic cliffs a thousand feet in height overhang the passage, at the bottom of which there is room for the rushing river, with grassy openings and groves of pine on either side. The forest and the wave alike teem with legged and winged game. Fish there are none to speak of, probably on account of the hot and mineral springs above, the effect of which is perceptible in the moderate (though not tepid) temperature of the water, the dense mists which arise from it in early morning, and the presence of certain aquatic plants along the bottom, which we (perhaps mistakenly) attributed to the warm springs above. The Lower Madison abounds in fish, and there is nothing to prevent them from ascending to this point, except the possible effect of the thermal waters.

We named no end of grand pinnacles and precipices in this beautiful cañon; but I fear our names will not stick. Doubtless Hayden or somebody came along afterward, with a dictionary and a reporter, and dubbed them all over again; and ere long the Plantation Bitters man, with his pot and brush, will have obliterated distinctions utterly, and labeled all the prominent points alike. It is with a sad presentiment, therefore, that I recall the glories of Cathedral Rock, where high in the air the basaltic columns strangely curve and meet to form in the face of the cliff the outline of a stately Gothic arch; or Pulpit Rock, a bold elevated rostrum after the fashion which Mr Beecher detests; or Thrasher's Hole, a gap in the western wall, through which was seen a fascinating amphitheater of wooded hills, and which got its name from the difficulty with which Thrasher, his mule, and his camera, were restrained from "going for it," to the infinite delay of the expedition; or Family Buttes, a magnificent series of jutting peaks and buttresses, terminating the cañon, beneath the shadow of which we made camp after the passage.

Our journey had not been altogether without stirring adventures, such as the christening of Duck Creek and the interview of Hardpan with a bear.

The way to christen a creek is to immerse something in it; and the article immersed, in this case, was a member of the party, who desires me to suppress his name. We were trotting along the river-bottom, when an inquisitive coyote, or prairie-wolf, poked his head over the terrace above us. A rifle-shot checked his curiosity without really frightening him much, and he kept pace with us upon his upper level in that graceful and leisurely way which characterizes his tribe, — the loafers of the wilderness. Sawtelle was suitably indifferent, as an old hunter should be, knowing well the small pecuniary value of a coyote-skin. But Sawtelle's dog raced after the trivial prey like mad; and two or three of us, realizing that any thing is game which gives you a good chase, sprang up the terrace in eager pursuit. Result: Mr. Coyote surveying us with calm wonder, out of rifle-range, and with the whole continent for his line of retreat; a brace of panting sportsmen, looking and feeling ridiculous; and, worst of all, Sawtelle's dog yelping away, with all the breath left in his body, after a dozen antelope that sailed away up the highland, alarmed by our too sudden emergence from below. There was nothing for it but an antelope-hunt by another relay of the party, and an ignominious return of the defeated ones to lead and drive the pack animals.

The gentleman to whom I have dimly alluded happened to have the task of leading an ambitious bay horse, to whose noble but somewhat broken-winded spirit the pack was an unaccustomed insult. As we pushed along the valley we came to a narrow, lively stream, across which most of us passed without difficulty. The docile steed which this gentleman rode waded peacefully through the flood, and the vicious beast he was leading "bucked" suddenly on the hither shore. He would not let go the leading rope, since that involved a long gallop after a runaway; and, firmly holding on, he exhorted the recusant in an inspiring tone to "git up and git!" Unfortunately exhortations are most heeded where not needed; the good horse got up and got, and the naughty horse sat down. Between the two, I found myself — I mean the anonymous gentleman found himself — suddenly disporting in the cool, cool wave. Blessings on those big Spanish stirrups out of which one slips so easily! So we christened it Duck Creek, and went our dripping way. Thank fortune, those fellows who went after antelope didn't get any that time! There is a damp kind of misery which can not bear to look upon success; and drying one's self at a gallop in a biting wind makes the temper as creaky as the joints.

The hero of Duck Creek was likewise he who climbed the dead cottonwood after a wounded eagle in its nest. Those who remained to scoff, under the tree, say it was beautiful to see him, embracing with legs and arms the wind-swayed trunk, proceed, after the fashion of a measuring-worm, while the bottoms of his pantaloons, catching the contagious upward tendency, traveled kneeward along his noble limbs faster than he skyward on the cottonwood. Four times that heroic being ascended in vain; four times he descended, with rapid friction, bringing much rotten and cotton wood: but the fifth time he carried up in his indomitable clinched teeth the end of a lariat, which he fastened around the tree, and then, descending in triumph, planted himself on a neighboring knoll, victoriously tetered out, and captured the shot eagle and two eaglets.

It was down at the camp on Bear Creek that Hardpan interviewed the bear. He was not hunting bear just at that time, but eating berries with both hands and all his might and mouth. A rustling in the bushes indicated the approach of a bear. He awaited the encounter with stern courage, resolved to stab the bear with his jack-knife at the moment of the fatal hug; for, in changing his position to get a better view of the foe, he had accidentally left behind his hat and his gun. It was a very large bear, to judge by the rustling in the bushes. In fact, continuing to judge, with that rapidity which brave men show in the face of danger, he judged that there were several of them, all large. Unfortunately, stepping across to a point about half a mile farther down the creek, to get a still better view, he lost so much time (a full minute and a half), that the bears escaped. In a solemn procession to the berrying-ground, we saw the very bushes that had rustled, and recovered the hat and rifle.

Our practice at night was to pour water on the fire after supper, and picket the animals close around us where we lay on the ground. After reaching the Upper Madison, we took turns in standing guard, to watch against possible stealing or stampeding of the stock, and also, from time to time, to see to it that the picket-ropes were clear. When you want to pasture one horse for one night on an ample lawn, the business is easy enough. You drive your picket-pin deep enough to hold, and leave enough of it above ground to permit the firm fastening of the rope, but not to permit the winding up of the rope on the pin by possible circular promenades on the horse's part; after which, you bid the horse, and all care on his behalf, good-night. Unless he is a very raw recruit at picket-duty, he will move about with perfect freedom over the whole circle of which the rope is the radius; and you will hear him nibble and crunch the squeaking grass at all hours of the night. But, when you apprehend Indians, you can't afford to hunt up a smooth lawn for each horse. As the higher mountains are entered, the grass grows scanty, and it is necessary to make the best of such patches as occur. So the animals get picketed where bushes interfere with the free circulation of the ropes, or so near together that they can (and accordingly do) get up mutual entanglements. Every such performance shortens the radius, and the realm of food. An experienced picketer generally makes one or two attempts to disentangle himself, by traveling around in the direction that first occurs to him. If this happens to be the right one, he may work out again to the full area of his destined supper: otherwise he winds himself up, and then (unlike a clock) stops going. It is the duty of the guard to go out, unwind him, and start him again, lest, standing in patient disgust all night, he be found in the morning empty of grass and of spirit for the day's work. It is solemnly amusing to march in a moony midnight hither and thither, followed by a silent steed, through all the intricacies of the knot he has tied, with the aid of stumps, bushes, his own legs, and his neighbor's rope. Fancy yourself unraveling a bad case of shoestring, and obliged to pull a horse through every loop at the end of the string. The "Lancers" is nothing to it. For a real mazy dance, to puzzle the floor-committee, give me the nine-horse picket-cotillion.

At daylight the animals are let loose, and stray about, trailing their long ropes, in search of untrampled grass for breakfast. It is easy to catch them by means of the ropes, though now and then an experienced old fellow has learned the exact length of his lariat, and will not let you get near enough to clutch the end of it.

This keeping guard at night without the companionship of the camp-fire is a chilly and dispiriting affair. The first watch is not very lonely. There is generally some wakeful comrade who sits up in his bed to talk ; or perhaps the whole party linger around the flameless embers, exchanging stories of adventure. But he who "goes on" from midnight till dawn, surrounded only by mummies rolled in blankets on the ground, is thrown upon his thoughts for company. The night-noises are mysterious and amazingly various, particularly if the camp is surrounded by woods. There are deer and elk going down to the water to drink; there are unnatural birds that whistle and answer, for all the world, like ambuscading savages; there are crackling twigs ; the picket-ropes crawl through the grass with a dreadful sound; the grass itself squeaks in an unearthly way when it is pulled by the horses' mouths. The steady crunching of their grinders is a re-assuring, because familiar sound; but ever and anon it stops suddenly, all the horses seeming to stand motionless, and to listen. Their ears are quicker than yours: they hear something moving in the forest, — doubtless the wily Sioux. You glide from tree to tree, revolver in hand, until you get near enough to see that they are all asleep. Old Bony is dreaming unpleasantly besides: it is an uncanny thing, — a horse with the nightmare. You make the rounds. They all wake and go to eating again: so you know they were not scared — except the blooded bay, who mistakes you for an Indian, and snorts and cavorts furiously.

I remember well such a night, near the banks of the Yellowstone Lake, when we were doubly suspicious, because we had heard a rifle-shot close by our camp, not fired by any member of our party. I was on guard at about one A.M., and keenly alive to all the blood-curdling sensations I have mentioned, when suddenly the trees above and the ground beneath were shaken by a brief but unmistakable earthquake. The shock was in the nature of a horizontal vibration; and the emotion produced by the experience at such an hour, in the solemn woods, was a unique combination of awe and nausea. I was not sorry that one or two of the party were waked by it: under the circumstances, I was grateful for a little conversation.

IV.

HOT-SPRINGS AND GEYSERS.

By our camp under Family Buttes, at the upper end of the third great Madison cañon, the river "forks;" a considerable stream, called the East Fork of the Madison, coming in at this point. We ascended this stream two or three miles, attracted by the appearance of a stream in the distance, which we found to proceed from a group of large hot-springs. These we studied with great zeal, and named with much ingenuity. Unfortunately, the greater wonders subsequently observed have driven these out of my memory; and one of my note-books, in which the whole thing is carefully recorded, with a view to immortality, is, at the moment of the present writing, in the pocket of my other coat; and I fear that coat has been surreptitiously sold by my wife, for pin-money, to a gentleman from Jerusalem who does business in our street; and at any rate I don't want the thing, and wouldn't use it if I had it. It is my impression that we called one spring the Caldron, another the Kettle, a third the Safety-Valve, a fourth the Reservoir, and a fifth the Devil's something or other. Necessity is generally the mother of profanity in the nomenclature of hot-springs. But I remember the

Bath-Tub, a deep crystal *Laug*, on the brim of which we sat, and parboiled our feet in the steaming tide, until, the action of the water having in some strange way thinned the aggregate cuticle, and increased the sensitiveness of the membrane left, the fear of blisters overcame the love of romance.

Probably none of these springs are active geysers, though one or two of the group may be so, and some of them boil with great vehemence. The Caldron, in particular, lifts a pyramid of ebullition, several feet in diameter, to the height, occasionally, of two feet. The most interesting feature of the group is the precipitation of iron in the quieter parts of their reservoirs. We could see, for instance, in the Bath-Tub, bubbles of steam ascending from many small vents at the bottom, indicating the points where the heated water from beneath came up. As the hot stream escaped from subterraneous pressure, and came in contact with the cooler water above, it apparently precipitated a portion of its iron (doubtless held in solution under pressure as bicarbonate); and this precipitation took place around the jet of hot water, so as to form a tube, from the upper end of which the hotter current continued to escape. The process goes on, of course, very slowly; and the tubes do not harden, but are flexible and slimy. In the largest reservoir they have accumulated great size, and lie along the bottom wherever the hottest currents have flowed. They look like reddish-brown slime-covered logs; but a little scientific investigation with a long pole dissipates at once the log and the illusion.

Returning to the main stream,—or rather the Fire-Hole River, since this is the name given to the western branch, from this point up,—we ascended its course southward. For a dozen miles it traverses a wild and narrow cañon, breaking through the mountain-range which forms one wall of the Madison cañon described in the last chapter. Our course lay up and down, and every whither; sometimes in the stream itself, when the steep precipices gave no footing; sometimes along a narrow grassy margin beneath the cliffs; sometimes straight up a fearful "climb;" sometimes straight down an awful slide; through the thick forests, over or around the fallen timber; Thrasher's mule playing fantastic tricks, with only a hand's-breadth between her and everlasting smash, with the ruin of American art as a consequence; the other animals occasionally infected with the desire of trying impossible passages, or of unloading themselves at any expense: but cool heads, and good temper, and the diamond hitch, were finally triumphant over all. It was a glorious, though a fatiguing, dozen miles. Several fine falls and rapids were passed; and frequently we left the trail, to steal out upon some projecting point, and gaze into the deep gorge, and the whirling, roaring, iridescent flood. The scenery of this region is never going to get justice from the critics. Everybody will rave about the geysers and the Yellowstone, and these lovely glades and wild ravines will be set down as ordinary in comparison. Nor can I afford to dally any longer by the way in this sentimental fashion. I must give up the itinerary style, and plunge at once, so to speak, into the hot-springs and geysers. And, before we go a step farther, I mean to get rid of a heavy weight of science which has burdened my soul long enough. You shall not see a single geyser till you have heard the geyser theory.

The word "geyser" is an Icelandic term, meaning to break forth: consequently, nothing is truly a geyser which is not truly a "buster." As Hardpan says, after seeing the genuine article in the Fire-Hole basin, "Those small sizzlers they call geysers in California might just as well dry up or simmer down: they can't run a two-for-a-bit side-show along of this!"

The true geyser, then, is characterized by a peculiar intermittent activity. It discharges periodically, with almost explosive force, a column of hot water and steam into the air; and, after the eruption is over, it remains quiet for a considerable time. Now, ask me four questions; to wit: Where does the water come from? What makes it hot? Why does it shoot into the air? Why does it stop shooting? — and don't bother me with cross-questionings; for this is a subject that will bear more explanation than discussion.

WONDERS OF THE YELLOWSTONE. 181

The water comes, no doubt, from the same source that supplies all ordinary springs; namely, the clouds. This is proved by the location of the geysers and hot-springs at the foot of mountains, &c., where the percolating waters would naturally find an outlet. How deeply they have penetrated, however, before they appear in their heated condition, it is impossible to say. The fact that the surface all around is cold, except when actually wet with the hot water, or permeated with hot gases, seems to indicate a deep origin of the heat. It is probable, however, that only a part, if any, of the percolating springs actually penetrate so far. At comparatively shallow depths they are probably met by ascending vapors from below, at intense temperatures, and thus heated to a mean degree.

According to some authors, the source of all this heat, like that of volcanoes and earthquakes, is cosmical; that is to say, the store of heat still remaining from the early incandescence of the earth, or, in other words, the fiery fluid interior of the globe. According to others, it is chemical, or the result of solutions and decompositions in underground deposits. That the latter cause is sufficient to account for vast degrees of heat, there is no doubt; though there is reason to believe that volcanic phenomena are due, in part at least, to wider causes, and that the solfataras, hot-springs, and geysers belong in the same class. My own observations incline me to believe that both the heat and the decomposition of subterranean rocks contribute to the temperature of thermal springs. In cases where waters contain much iron, sulphuric acid, sulphureted hydrogen, or alkalies, a considerable decomposition of the rocks may be plausibly inferred. When, however, as in most of the geysers of the Madison, the water contains little mineral matter, and that mostly silica, it is difficult to give an adequate chemical cause of the heat, without assuming boldly that the results of decomposition have been precipitated on their way up to the surface.

The peculiar discharge of the geysers, and their still more remarkable intermittency, is the result of the geyser tube and its connection. A thermal spring, particularly a silicious one, tends to form for itself a mound by the evaporation of its continual overflow; and through the center of this mound runs, more or less vertical and regular, the channel or tube of the spring, branching off at the bottom into the duct or ducts through which the water is supplied. It has been supposed that the intermittent action of the geysers was due to subterranean reservoirs in which steam accumulated until its force was sufficient to cause an explosion; but Bunsen showed, nearly twenty-five years ago, that the tube itself is sufficient to account for all these irregularities. His experiments were made upon the Great Geyser in Iceland, the tube of which is from ten to eighteen feet in diameter, and has been probed to a depth of seventy or seventy-five feet. He ascertained the temperature of

WONDERS OF THE YELLOWSTONE. 183

the water at various parts of the tube just before an explosion, and found that, strange to say, it was nowhere boiling hot. This expression requires some explanation. Our phrase "boiling hot" does not signify any particular temperature. In the first place different liquids boil at very different heats. Ether and alcohol boil long before water: mercury, and most other fluids familiar to us in daily life, require a much higher temperature. If we were to try to boil mercury in a lead or tin spoon, the spoon would melt before the mercury would boil. But, even with one and the same liquid, the boiling-point depends on the pressure. Water may be heated in a closed vessel to 400° without boiling. Our boiling point of 212° Farenheit is the temperature at which water boils at the level of the sea at a barometric pressure of thirty inches of mercury. As we ascend in altitude, the temperature of boiling water decreases.

The boiling-point for any pressure is the temperature of saturated steam at that pressure. Assuming the altitude of the geyser basin at about sixty-five hundred feet, we have (23.64 inches barometer) 200° for the temperature of the water at boiling-point. At different depths in the geyser tube, when it is full of water, we have (by rough calculation) the following boiling-points: —

Ten feet, 216°; twenty feet, 229°; thirty feet, 240°; forty feet, 250°; fifty feet, 258°; sixty feet, 266°; seventy feet, 273°; one hundred feet (if the tube is so deep) 290°; four hundred feet, 380° (about a hundred and eighty-five pounds' pressure); one thousand feet, 452°, or about 453 pounds' per square inch.

Now, if the water at forty feet from the surface is, say, 245° hot, it can not boil; but, if any thing could move it up to thirty feet, it would there begin to boil, and give off steam vigorously, because it would be several degrees above the boiling temperature for that depth. The pressure at forty feet from the water in the tube is thirty pounds per inch; and that of the steam (at 245°), only about twenty-seven pounds. But at thirty feet the hydrostatic pressure is only twenty-five pounds; and hence, if the water at forty feet were pushed up to this point, it would be hot enough to fly into steam, and the steam would have two pounds' surplus pressure. The column of water above would, therefore, be lifted. If it were entirely lifted, so that the whole tube above thirty feet were full of steam, moving upward, the pressure upon the water below would be greatly reduced, and this would fly into steam with still greater excess of power. Practically, the two operations take place simultaneously; and from the middle, upward and downward, the whole geyser tube bursts into steam, and blows its contents out with great force.

The necessary preliminary lifting of the geyser column is effected by portions of steam, generated at the hottest points in the side-ducts, and forcing their way into the main tube. Here they meet with cooler water, by which they are condensed, unless, before that takes place, they lift the whole column enough to cause an eruption. The entrance, condensation, and collapse of these bodies of steam, may be distinguished at the surface by a sudden "jump," and subsidence again of the water in the geyser-pool over the tube, accompanied by explosive reports from below. Tyndall aptly calls these movements abortive eruptions. After numerous repetitions of them, during which the water in the tube reaches its maximum heat throughout, some larger lift than usual hoists the whole affair with its own petard, and it becomes the inquisitive observer to stand clear.

The duration of an eruption depends upon the amount of sufficiently hot water "banked up" in the subterranean channels which supply it. Its conclusion is marked by a diminution of steam pressure in the tube and a condensation of the remaining steam, causing a suction downward, which draws back the water from the surface-pool.

V.

THE LOWER GEYSER-BASIN OF THE FIRE-HOLE.

WE approached the geyser-basin with our expectation at the boiling-point, and ready to discharge; for we had among the baggage two copies of "Scribner's," containing Mr. Langford's account of the wonders of the region, as seen by the Washburne exploring party. His article occupied two numbers, and we had two copies of each: so four persons could be accommodated with intellectual sustenance at one time. For the other two, it was, as one of them mournfully observed, "Testaments, or nothin'."

Mr. Langford's articles (see "Scribner's" for May and June, 1871) were vivid and fascinating; and we found them, in the end, highly accurate. At the outset, however, we were inclined to believe them somewhat exaggerated; and Thrasher was divided between his desire to catch an instantaneous view of a spouting column two hundred and fifty-six feet high, and his ambition to prove, by the relentless demonstration of photography, that these vents of steam and hot water were "not half as big as they had been cracked up to be."

We were not at first aware that there are two geyser-basins on the Fire-Hole River; the upper one, ten miles above the other, being the smaller, but containing the largest geysers. It was this one which Washburne's party, coming from Yellowstone Lake, first stumbled upon, and, after viewing its splendid display, naturally passed by the inferior basin with little notice. But we, emerging from the forest, and finding ourselves on the border of a great gray plain, with huge mounds in the distance, from which arose perpetually clouds of steam, supposed we had reached the great sensation, and prepared to be enthusiastic or cynical as circumstances might dictate.

We rode for a mile across the barren plain, picking our way to avoid the soft places. This is quite necessary in the neighborhood of the hot-springs. Where they have deposited a white, hard crust, it is generally strong enough to bear horse and man; but, over large areas, the ground is like what we call, in the East, "spring-holes;" and the treacherous surface permits uncomfortable slumping through, haply into scalding water. It is not very deep; but a small depth under such circumstances is enough to make a fellow "suffer some," like the "lobster in the lobster-pot."

The plain contains a few scattered springs; and along the river, its western border, there are many in active ebullition. The principal group of geysers is at the upper or southern end, extending for some distance up the valley of a small tributary from the east. With cautious daring, we rode up the side of the great white mound, winding among the numerous fissures, craters, and reservoirs that on every side of us hissed, gurgled, or quietly vapored, with now and then a slight explosion, and a spurt to the height of a dozen feet or more. Sawtelle's dog nosed suspiciously around several of the basins, until, finding one that seemed not too hot for a bath, he plunged in, and emerged in a great hurry, with a yelp of disapprobation.

A couple of dead pines stood, lonesome enough, in the side of the hill, "whence all the rest had fled." — They had died at their posts, and to the said posts we made fast our horses, and ascended a few rods farther, until we stood by the borders of the summit springs. There were two or three large vents at the bottom of deep reservoirs or intricate caverns. It gives one an unpleasant thrill, at first, to hear the tumult of the imprisoned forces, and to feel their throes and struggles shaking the ground beneath one's feet; but this soon passes away, and the philosopher is enabled to stand with equanimity on the rim of the boiling flood, or even to poke his inquisitive nose into some dark fissure, out of which, perhaps, in a few moments more a mass of uproarious liquid and vapor will burst forth.

We lingered much longer in this basin than my brief notice of it indicates; for, you see, we thought we had found *the* geysers; and oh the hours that we spent "identifying" the individual springs that

Langford had described! Since the largest eruptions we observed did not exceed forty-five feet in height, we set down his account as hugely overdrawn, and were deeply disgusted at the depravity of travelers. But Sawtelle remarked, in his quiet way, that, "if it were not for that there article in that there magazine, these yer springs would be considered a big thing, after all; and perhaps it was just as well to let the magazine go to thunder, and enjoy the scenery." This sensible advice we followed with much profit and pleasure; and we are all now ready to admit that our happening upon the wrong lot of geysers first was a most fortunate occurrence, since we should otherwise have been tempted to pass them by as insignificant. The truth is, that, in some of the elements of beauty and interest, the lower basin is superior to its more startling rival. It is broader, and more easily surveyed as a whole; and its springs are more numerous, though not so powerful. Nothing can be lovelier than the sight, at sunrise, of the white steam-columns, tinged with rosy morning, ascending against the background of the dark-pine woods and the clear sky above. The variety in form and character of these springs is quite remarkable. A few of them make faint deposits of sulphur, though the greater number appear to be purely silicious. One very large basin (forty by sixty feet) is filled with the most beautiful slime, varying in tint from white to pink, which blobs and spits away, trying to boil, like a heavy theologian forcing a laugh to please a friend, in spite of his natural specific gravity. We called it the Paint-Vat; and Hayden's people, I see, have called it the Mud-Puff. Paint-Mud, or Puff-Vat, or any other permutation or combination, will do.

A geyser in its old age becomes a quiet, deep pool, or *laug*. This may occur by reason of the choking of the vent, or the gradual growth in altitude of the mound or tube, so that the hydrostatic pressure perpetually prevents explosive discharges; or any other cause leading to the opening of some new vent in its neighborhood; or, finally, a local diminution of the heat, a change in the subterranean channels by which the heated vapors reach the spring-water, or such an excess of the water-supply as prevents any part of it from being converted into steam. In Hayden's report it is suggested that the geyser eruptions must be most frequent and grand in the spring and autumn, when the supply of water is most abundant. It is possible, however, that a large and sudden supply of water may render them less frequent, or less grand, or both.

The *laugs*, or extinct geysers, are the most beautiful objects of all. Around their borders the white incrustations form quaint arabesques and ornamental bosses, resembling petrified vegetable growths. (At the risk of spoiling the rhetorical effort of this passage, I will boldly say that they most frequently look like sponges and cauliflowers.) The sides of the reservoir are corrugated and indented fancifully, like the recesses and branching passages of a fairy cavern. The water is brightly but not deeply blue. Over its surface curls a light vapor; through its crystal clearness one may gaze, apparently, to unfathomable depths; and, seen through this wondrous medium, the white walls seem like silver, ribbed and crusted with pearl. When the sun strikes across the scene, the last touch of unexpected beauty is added. The projected shadow of the decorated edge reveals by contrast new glories in the depths: every ripple on the surface makes marvelous play of tint and shade on the pearly bottom. One half expects to see a lovely naiad emerge with floating grace from her fantastically-carven covert, and gayly kiss her snowy hand through the blue wave. What we did see, in one such romantic instance, was the whitened skeleton of a mountain buffalo. Was it a case of disappointed love, and suicide? We voted otherwise, in our degraded cynicism, and decided that the old fool had come down from the hills to "take a little something hot," lost his footing (as folks will, who do that sort of thing), and got drowned, like Duke Clarence, in his own toddy. "Served him right," says Hardpan: "there was too much water in his drink." Whatever may be the moral of it, no king or saint was ever more magnificently entombed. Not the shrine of St. Antony of Padua, with its white marbles and its silver lamps, is so resplendent as this sepulcher in the wilderness. Thrasher thought it would make an elegant view, and would "take" amazingly as part of a stereopticonical exhibition, being a great natural curiosity. Everybody knows flies in amber; but who ever heard of a buffalo in sapphire? Still, there are some things which Thrasher can not do; and of these there are a very few which he will not even attempt. One of them is to stand astride of a deep pool of hot water, greater in diameter than the length of his legs, hold up a camera, and take a flying shot at a sub-aqueous buffalo. With unutterable woe in his countenance, he pronounced the unaccustomed words, "It can't be done," and was with difficulty prevented from taking a drink of collodion (by mistake) in his despair.

It was not until we had crossed the mountains to the Yellowstone that we discovered, through the courtesy of Lieut. Doane, whom we met upon that river, that we had not seen the grandest of the geysers. So, from the Great Cañon we struck straight across the ranges by a new route, and, emerging upon the Fire-Hole, followed it to the upper basin.

VI.

THE UPPER GEYSER-BASIN OF THE FIRE-HOLE.

THE centers of the two geyser-basins are about ten miles apart; though the distance along the river between them, in which no springs are found, does not exceed two or three miles. It is a lovely ride, fringed with groves made musical by the rippling stream, and watched over by the grandeur of the far hills. For a part of the way, the traveler winds along the slopes of vast accumulations of disintegrated geyser-sinter, like ashes, only stained in various colors with sulphur and iron, and mineral salts. At one place, several enormous hot-springs, which have built themselves up on the river-bank, unite to pour over their incrusted rim a steaming cascade into the main current. But such sights are grown familiar to us by this time, and we do not even ford the stream to take a closer look at them.

Just as we were about entering the upper basin, some quick eye caught sight of four strange spots on the side of a snowy geyser-mound in the distance ahead. They looked like so many dark paddles laid in a row; but we recognized them, with a thrill of anticipated feasting, as wild geese, lying, with their necks extended, to comfortably snooze and simmer in the sun. It is not a common thing to catch wild geese asleep: so we made preparations to terminate slumber with slaughter. The bold Hardpan and the wise ———, like Diomed and Ulysses in the glorious tenth book of the Iliad, "both lay down without the path," and wriggled towards the enemy's camp, while all the rest of us Greeks awaited the result. There was a long interval of silence, broken only by the occasional crackling of a twig. We learned subsequently that Ulysses insisted on crawling half a mile or so upon his stomach, and made the impetuous Tydides Hardpan do the same. At length the two belligerents emerged from the forest, in serpentine stillness, on the river-bank, just opposite the Trojans, who slept serenely, but at long range. Our warriors, sprawled at full-length, and stretching out their heads as far as their limited necks would allow, to reconnoiter the position, resembled ludicrously their sleeping victims. The gleam of two rifle-barrels was seen; a sharp double report broke the stillness; some white dust flew from the distant mound — and eighty pounds Troy weight of uninjured goose-flesh got up hastily, and went squawking down stream. As the discomfited sportsmen returned, Hardpan remarked, with assumed cheerfulness, that, by Jove, he had scared 'em some! But this paltry consolation availed nothing with the well-grieved Greeks. So, our experiment in the Homeric line being a failure, we shot a couple of ordinary ducks for dinner, and rode meekly forward.

A short distance farther brought us into the Upper Basin. This is about three miles long by half a mile wide. Entering at the lower end, and passing numerous quiescent springs, we recognized at once the cone of the Giant Geyser, which rises about ten feet above the surface of a low mound, and looks like the petrified hollow stump of a big tree. Riding by it a few hundred yards over the white sinter that covered the ground, we camped in the edge of a grove, almost under the shadow of the architectural pile of the Castle Geyser. But, while we were removing packs and saddles, a roar from the north indicated some unusual occurrence; and, looking thither, we saw the Giant in full activity. A few moments brought us to the spot; and approaching the geyser on the windward side, to escape the driving spray, we were able to examine it closely. Out of its throat, five feet in diameter, was rushing a full column of mingled steam and water, the latter rising a hundred feet (by measurement taken of a less than maximum height), and the former shooting cloudily much higher, and then drifting away with the wind. This monstrous eruption lasted three hours; and during its continuance the volume of the river into which the water flowed was nearly doubled.

A dozen feet from the main cone was a small vent, which for a long time only vapored quietly, like a meditative teakettle. Suddenly, however, this small side-vent began to blow off steam with considerable noise and power, and immediately the force of the Giant Geyser was perceptibly weakened. This was a safety-valve, or rather a low-water detector such as we attach to steam-boilers. When the water sunk to a certain level under ground, the steam escaped through this side-channel, and thus the pressure in the main tube was weakened. We thought the eruption was about to come to a close; but new accessions of steam and water below revived its enthusiasm, the safety-valve shut up again, and the column rose to its former height, this process being several times repeated during the long continuance of the spring's activity.

Near the Giant is the Grotto, — a geyser which has covered over its cone, so that the vent is partly horizontal. Some of us put our heads in, and could see the boiling and muttering water about twenty feet below. One of the party proposed to crawl through the cavern of sinter, with irregular side-openings, which housed this spring; but he was fortunately dissuaded. If he had tried it, he would have been a parboiled man, and of no further use to anybody, except to point a paragraph of soul-harrowing description in this article, and to stop that hole against some other fool, until the operation of time and hot water had reduced him to the merely ornamental condition of a skeleton, like that of the buffalo lately described, — the only insoluble things about him being his bones, and how they got there. For the geyser suddenly began to play, and a scalding stream poured from the openings just now so safe and dry.

This geyser also had its safety-valve companion, in fact, more than one of them. The one which most attracted us was a deep and beautiful reservoir, into which ran one of the streams from the gushing Grotto. Supposing that the reservoir was thus being filled, we placed a pebble on the margin at the water's edge, that we might measure the rate of its rise; but returning in eight minutes, we found, to our surprise, that the water had fallen a foot. The geyser was emptying the reservoir from below, while it returned but a portion of its contents by the surface stream we had noticed. One of the scientific gentlemen said he knew all about it, it was in Greenleaf's Arithmetic: "A cistern has two spouts: one is able to fill it in one hour, and the other will empty it in half an hour. Now, if the diameter of the cistern be 173,258,421 feet, and the height 25,479,623 feet, and the weight of the water 62.49 pounds per cubic foot, and the rate of legal interest six per cent, and both spouts be running, how long will it take to fill the cistern?" He said it was only necessary to substitute x and y for some of these quantities, to make the case apply to the Grotto Geyser; and he promised to work the thing out for me when we got home. But now he says that part of his Greenleaf has been torn out; and, besides, he is sure it is one of those things "that no fellow can find out," because it depends on the amount of water, which varies with the reports of the Signal Service Bureau.

After we returned to camp, Old Faithful, in many respects the most beautiful geyser of all, gave us a brief but very satisfactory exhibition. This geyser is situated near the upper end of the basin, upon the top of a symmetrical mound; and its tube, being smooth and vertical, gives a remarkably straight and perfect jet, rising, sometimes, to the height of two hundred feet. The performance of Old Faithful lasts only about twenty minutes; but it is repeated generally every hour. It was in full sight from camp, and we could admire it at our ease, without leaving our late and welcome dinner. A lively breeze carried the white steam away to one side, and left a clean, sharp, vertical edge on the other side, marking against the woods and the sky the column of the fountain, and giving to the whole the appearance of a gigantic plume. At intervals during the night we turned our heads, without rising, as we heard Old Faithful's booming signal, and beheld through the trees the pillar of cloud, snow-white and sparkling in the starry night.

Probably the geysers are not regular in their times of eruption. The Great Geyser of Iceland is notoriously lazy and whimsical; and often parties are obliged to leave without having seen it discharge at all, after camping and watching beside it for many days. In our American geyser-basins, the springs are so numerous, that no one fails to see at least a dozen eruptions, though the largest are not the most frequent. Here is a list of some of the principal geysers of the Upper Basin, as seen by Washburne's, Hayden's, or our party. The heights have been determined by actual though sometimes rude measurement; but it must be borne in mind that they generally represent the maximum observed. Some of the geysers maintain this maximum height with surprising steadiness: others rapidly diminish in power.

Giant. — Diameter, 5 feet; height, 140 feet; lasts 3 hours.

Giantess. — Diameter, 18 feet; height of small jet, 250 feet; lasts 20 minutes.

Beehive. — Diameter, 2 feet; height, 219 feet; lasts 20 minutes.

Grand Geyser. — Diameter, 6 feet; height, 200 feet; lasts 20 minutes.

Old Faithful. — Diameter, 20 inches; height, 200 feet; lasts 20 minutes.

Grotto. — Diameter, 4 feet; height, 60 feet; lasts 30 minutes.

Castle. — Diameter, 3 feet; height, 50 feet.

Fan. — Height, 60 feet; lasts 10 to 30 minutes.

Besides these, there are numerous geysers throwing their jets from ten to forty feet, and many springs which bear every indication of being geysers, though they have not yet been observed in violent action.

A still larger number have once been geysers, and have now relapsed into the quiet old age of the *laug*, or have never been geysers, but hope to be some day, when they have accumulated a tube of sufficient height,—just as boys, when I was a boy, looked forward to the achievements of manhood as synonymous with the possession of high standing-collars.

It was hard for us to tear ourselves away from this interesting region; but duty called, and lack of provisions and ammunition induced us to listen. So, from the Upper Basin we went back to Virginia City, by forced marches, in four days, at the rate of over thirty miles a day. Our homeward journey was enlivened by one small "Indian encounter," which, if I should embellish it after the manner of frontier historians, would cause the sympathetic scalps of many a Christian household to tingle. But "my conscience, hanging about the neck of my heart," bids me confess that there was no fighting done, and that our running was executed with dignified firmness.

This is not all of my story; for I shall go back, as the novelists do, and take up the thread of the tale in the middle thereof, narrating in my next chapter our experiences of the great lake, cañon, and cataracts of the Yellowstone.

VII.

YELLOWSTONE LAKE AND RIVER.

The great lake from which the Yellowstone River flows is about twenty-two miles long from north to south, and ten to fifteen miles wide from east to west. Several long peninsulas extend into it from the southern shore; so that the shape of the lake has been compared to a human hand. The imaginative gentleman who discovered this resemblance must have thought the size and form of fingers to be quite insignificant, provided the number was complete. The hand in question is afflicted with elephantiasis in the thumb, dropsy in the little finger, hornet-bites on the third finger, and the last stages of starvation in the other two. There are several islands in the lake; and soundings taken at many points indicate a depth nowhere exceeding fifty fathoms. The altitude above sea-level is 7,427 feet.

The scene presented to our eyes by this lake, as we emerged from the thick forests on the western side, and trod with exultation its sandy shore, was indeed lovely. The broad expanse of shining water, the wooded banks and bosky islands, the summits of lofty mountains beyond it, faintly flushed with sunset, the deep sky, and the perfect solitude and silence, combined to produce a memorable impression.

We camped near a group of hot springs, in one of which we cooked our beans for breakfast by suspending the kettle over night in the boiling tide. Beans take a good while to "do," especially at such altitudes, where the temperature of boiling water is many degrees lower than at sea-level. We regarded this piece of cookery, therefore, as a culinary triumph.

Near our camp was another hot-spring, illustrating in a curious way the precipitation of silica, to which I have alluded in previous articles. The water emerged at high temperature from a vent in the bottom of the lake two or three feet from the shore. Coming in contact with the cold water of the lake, it lost so much heat by the mixture as to be forced to precipitate its silica; but this precipitation had always taken place at a certain distance from the vent. In the course of time, therefore, a wall of silica had been built up through the lake-water, like a coffer-dam; so that now the hot spring was completely protected against the cold water, and stood in the lake like a basin, with its surface several inches above the lake-surface, and its hot current spilling over this self-constructed brim. On the shore-side there was no such wall.

The lake swarms with salmon-trout, weighing from one to four pounds each. Many of them are afflicted with a curious intestinal worm, of a different species from the two which are already recognized as parasites of the salmon genus in Europe. Too many of these tape-worms are not good for a trout; but five or six do not seem to hurt him much. We had no difficulty in rejecting, from the great number which we caught with hook and line in a short time, such as were unfit for food. The wormy fellows bite the best, which is strange, when one considers that they have already more bait in them than is wholesome.

Thrasher was wild with enthusiasm about the views to be obtained from every point around the lake; and it took the whole company to tear him away from each successive promontory. By judiciously indulging him on occasions of peculiar importance, however, we succeeded in bringing him to the outlet, at the north-west corner of the lake, where the Yellowstone proper begins. Here we camped in a beautiful grove commanding a prospect of the lake, woods, mountains, and river, so lovely as to linger yet in my memory, — the last and the fairest picture of all. About six miles below the lake, and again at eight miles, there are groups of sulphur-springs and "mud-volcanoes." The presence of sulphur in these waters leads to the formation of numerous salts, such as alum, &c., and the precipitation by sublimation of beautiful specimens of crystallized sulphur. These are very fragile; and it severely taxed the ingenuity of our party to pack them, in the absence of suitable materials, so as to safely transport them. ("The absence of materials" *is* very poor stuff to pack things in, as you will find out if you try it.)

It was while venturing, in search of specimens, too near the edge of a vehemently bubbling and roaring caldron, that Thrasher slumped through the thin crust, and took a steam-and-sulphur bath up to his waist. He scrambled out so quickly, however, that he suffered no apparent effects, unless we were right in attributing to chemical re-actions the increased spottiness of his corduroys.

The largest "mud volcano," or geyser, is situated on a steep hillside, and surrounded with trees. The crater is about forty feet in diameter at the top, and contracts rapidly to less than half that size. By cautiously approaching the edge, and seizing the opportunity when the steam drifts away, a view may be obtained of the dingy and dismal interior. At the depth of about thirty feet may be seen the surface of the boiling mass, consisting of very thin mud in the most violent agitation. We saw nothing like an eruption; and the only proof of such an occurrence is the condition of the surrounding trees, some of which have been killed, while others (even young and growing trees) are covered more or less with mud.

About eighteen miles below the lake, the Yellowstone plunges from its high level into the upper cañon. Only a few rapids give warning of the approaching change. The river runs between low but steep, and sometimes vertical rocky banks, until, bursting through a narrow gateway, it leaps down in a fine cataract a hundred and forty feet. Thence it flows tumultuously onward (re-enforced by Cascade Creek, which tumbles into it from the West), through a picturesque cañon, for about one-third of a mile; and then comes the grand cataract, three hundred and fifty feet in one unbroken plunge. The surface of the country around rather increases than diminishes in altitude as we follow the river down. The cañon is carved in it; and the banks rise from twelve hundred to fifteen hundred feet above the river in the bottom.

A curious architectural effect is given to the scene by the peculiar form of the cañon. The material of the country just below the falls is largely composed of soft clays, sand, tufa, volcanic ash and breccia, &c., with occasional masses (layers or boulders) of basalt and other harder rocks. In this soft material the agencies of rain, frost, and mountain-streams, have wrought effectively. Every little brook or temporary stream that spills into the Yellowstone at this point from the surrounding highlands has cut a deep notch of its own; and between these side-gulches great buttresses are left standing in the main cañon. These would soon be carried away by the surface-sweeping agencies mentioned, but for the fact that their forces toward the river are protected by terminal rock-masses too hard to be thus disintegrated and removed. But their upper surfaces, between these termini and the main bank, are sometimes deeply degraded, so that the rocky points stand like pinnacles. We went out upon one or two of them, first descending somewhat, then traversing a narrow neck (about a yard wide, with a precipice on either hand), and then climbing up to the pinnacle. The feat is more perilous in appearance than in reality; for the soft, ashy material gives excellent footing, and, even if one slipped, one might slide to the bottom without injury. Standing upon the pinnacle is far more trying to the nerves. Here one finds one's self upon a rock not larger than a dinner-table, with an almost vertical precipice of more than a thousand feet on three sides, and a slim connection with *terra firma* on the fourth. Most people prefer, under the circumstances, to sit down: so at least did we, and gathered composure by a brief rest, before giving ourselves up to the contemplation of one of the most magnificent scenes on earth.

From our point of observation we command a view of several miles of the cañon. To the north, it soon disappears by a sharp turn, and penetrates gloomier scenes. We can see the black walls that overhang, far away, its awful depths. Southward, and beneath and around us, there is no gloom, but grandeur steeped in glory. A thousand feet below us, the river, tiny in the distance, stretches its ribbon of emerald, embroidered with silver foam. The great walls of the cañon glow with barbaric splendor, in such hues as Nature's palette seldom furnishes. The bright yellow of the sulphury clay is splashed with blood-red stains of iron, and striped here and there with black bands of lava. It is the "Schwarz — Roth — Gold" of the ancient German banner, than which there never was or will be a more gorgeous blazonry. Above it the dark pine-woods finish the picture with a green fringe against the blue depths of the sky; and, as the eye ranges up the long line of crested pinnacles and shining precipices, it rests at last upon the snowy column of the distant cataracts. It is too far away to make its warning heard. This is the banquet of the eye, and the ear is not invited. In the clear, upper air we approach the perfect stillness of which the poet sings, — "that lucid interspace 'twixt world and world," where dwell the gods,

"Nor sound of human sorrow mounts to mar
Their secret, everlasting calm."

To bid farewell to such a scene is like descending from the heights of heaven. Precious indeed is the memory of so fair a vision, yet blent forever with the pain of yearning. O silent splendors of solitude! shall we never greet you again? Verily, not as before; for ye are now part of a National Park, and ye have a superintendent, and are speedily to be provided with a turnpike and a hotel, and daily stages connecting with the railroad; and, when we revisit you, we shall pay toll to the man who owns the staircase at the pinnacle; and the fair being who leans upon our arm will view the scene through her lorgnette, and say it is not so nice as Niagara, and hurry us away.

THE ICE-CAVES OF WASHINGTON TERRITORY.

NO ice! Disconsolate drinkers hung about the bar-rooms, sipping insipid cocktails and cobblers, or playing "freeze out" in grim irony, to decide who should have the first lump out of that refrigerant cargo daily expected from the North. Butter pathetically swam about on the platters; cucumbers visibly wilted for disappointed hope; fresh meat grew prematurely old with sorrow; the ice-cream shebangs shut up their business, and all over town might be heard the diabolical chuckle and supercilious snuffle of the tea-kettles, celebrating the triumph of hot water over cold. Even the Templars couldn't stand it. That worthy association had no scruples about appropriating the convivial songs of all ages, and skillfully injecting "cold water" into the place originally occupied by "ruby wine," to adapt them for the uses of reform; but the strongest stomach in the fraternity rebelled at the Bacchanalian choruses, "*Warm* water for me!" "Tepid and bright in its liquid light," "In the simmering stream our brows we lave, and parboil our lips in the crystal wave." For once, the all-transforming wand of the Muse of Temperance was powerless, and the melodeon of the Lodge "dried up." This was the situation at Portland, Or.; and it was, to borrow the most expressive word in the Chinook jargon, — that ripest fruit of time, product of all languages, essence of concentrated speech, — it was, I say, *cultus:* yes, *hyas cultus*, or, in feeble Saxon, highly inconvenient, disgusting, demoralizing.

Happy Dalles City, meanwhile, reveled in ice. The living were content, the unburied dead were comfortable, and topers were saved the additional sin of profanity; for the seductive bar-room sign of "Iced Mixed Drinks" was not a taunting, fraudulent voice crying in the sage-brush. The philosophic observer, inquiring as to the cause of this strange contrast, was informed that a mysterious ice-cave in Washington Territory constituted a reserve upon which the Dalles fell back in seasons when the improvidence of the Oregonians, and some unusual irregularity in climate, combined, exhausted the supply of the great necessity of civilized life.

Moved by various individual motives, but united in the desire to render thanks at headquarters for this blessed relief, a small party of us formed the plan of an excursion to the cave. There was a keen and portly Portlander, who cherished a secret intention of building a hotel, constructing a wagon-road, and creating out of the cave a fashionable ice-watering-place. There was a young, enthusiastic tourist from the Mississippi Valley, who, having lived out West till the West was East, had come to explore the veritable Occident, beyond which there is none. There was a veteran inhabitant, who goes out every spring on snow-shoes, and "claims" the cave, under an ingenious application of mining law, as a mineral deposit, so as to obtain a monopoly of the ice-packing business. And, finally, there was the present writer, a person habitually animated by the purest impulses known to reconstructed humanity, who joined the party because he wished to do so, than which no reason could be more conclusive, or free from base motives.

As we disembarked from the handsome steamer of the Oregon Steam Navigation Company, near the mouth of the White Salmon, we found ourselves assembled upon the sandy bank, as follows: four men, four horses, and a huge quantity of bacon, crackers, &c., together with a pair of blankets apiece. The work of distributing the baggage, and packing it behind our saddles, so that it would not pound on a trot, nor rattle on a gallop, nor quietly slip off on a walk, so that the matches would not ignite upon the coffee-pot, nor the bacon flavor the sugar, nor the sardines burst among the crackers, nor the candles (for exploring the cave) be mangled by the knives and spoons (for exploring the victuals), was not accomplished without some difficulty. But at length all was adjusted except the frying-pan, which would not pack, and was accepted by the Veteran, with some profane grumbling, as a very unnecessary evil, which ought by rights to be "slung to thunder," but was unjustly slung to him instead. That frying-pan owes its safety throughout our trip to the fact that it was borrowed, and must be returned. The Veteran rode ahead, brandishing it sullenly, like some new instrument of warfare, and we followed in single file.

It was a ride of some forty miles to the cave, through the bewildering beauty and grandeur of the Cascade Mountains. We galloped over high, breezy table-lands; we looked down on Josselin's nestling ranch, alive with cattle, and lovely with fruit-laden orchards; we followed the narrow trail along the steep mountain-side, the deep misty cañon of the White Salmon below us, and beyond it the leafy mountains rising, ridge above ridge, until they were veiled in the smoke of burning forests far away. We threaded our way through thick wildernesses of undergrowth, parting the branches with our hands, and scarcely able to see before us the path, well worn for the feet by patient pack-mules, but not yet quite ready for a rider taller than a bundle of ice. Anon we emerged into beautiful openings carpeted with bunch-grass or wild oats, and dotted with stately oaks and pines, the ground kept smooth and lawny by woodland fires, that creep silently from tuft to tuft of grass or dry leaves, or smolder along the course of fallen trunks, and kiss with burning, deceitful passion, as they pass, the feet of the giants of the forest, that disdain to notice such trifles while they can look abroad upon a measureless world and sky. But now and then, favored by drought and wind, the creeping fires grow bold, and spring like tigers upon some feeble, dry old tree, wrapping it in flame from root to crown; or they gnaw at a sturdy trunk till its strength is undermined, and then, some fair, quiet day, like that on which we rode through these solitudes, the overstrained column gives way suddenly, and — with a groan, a rustle of unavailing resistance, a vain wringing of leafy hands, and wild tossing of rugged arms, a crackling, a crashing, a great rush and sweep, and a final heavy boom as of far artillery, waking the echoes of the pitying hills — a tree falls! Beautiful, but ah! how sad, were the belief, that imprisoned within it was a conscious Dryad — conscious, but not immortal — to feel her life carried downward in that mighty fall, into the hopeless abyss of annihilation; or, sadder yet, to lie thereafter prone in the forest, and wait the deliverance even of utter destruction at the merciful hands of Time and Decay!

But now we stand upon the crest of a high, steep ridge, down which, with slow and careful steps, we must lead our horses. At the bottom rushes the swift White Salmon, which we cross upon a frail, swaying bridge to climb the rocky height upon the other side, and mount again to gallop through the woods. West of the river the surface rises in irregular terraces, the results of successive basaltic overflows. The rocky ridges, peeping through the soil, cross our path at intervals; and the fine dust rising from the trail beneath our horses' feet is the same in character as that which daily chases the wagons on the roads over the vast volcanic highlands between the Columbia and the Snake. These rugged outcrops are the haunts of the graceful rattlesnake and the vivacious yellow-jacket. My acquaintance with one individual of the latter, though brief, was long enough to be fatal to him, and memorable to me. Our party was quietly jogging through the forest, and my eyes were fixed, with mild lack of interest, upon the crupper of the steady beast that bore the tourist, when suddenly that respectable charger stopped, tried to kick with all his feet at once, reared, plunged, bucked, and revolved his tail with furious rapidity in a plane at right angles with the axis of his body. A moment after, my own steed began a similar series of antics, under the attacks of a host of little bandits in golden mail, whose retreat we had invaded. I laughed aloud at the novel situation; but the insult was terribly avenged. Straight out of the empty air came a raging cavalier to answer the challenge, and we fought it out in half a second. He insisted on his right to choose ground, weapons, and distance; to wit, my hand, his sting, and considerably less than nothing. His arrangements were so well made that he was well "into" me before I got "onto" him. Result: one small dead yellow-jacket, of no account whatever, and a hand and arm nearly as useless. I "gained flesh" for an hour with astonishing speed — losing sight of knuckles and sinews; and, had I that day presented my hand to an aged, purblind father, he would have had cause to say, "The voice is the voice of Jacob; but the hand is the hand of the boy in Pickwick." Some good whiskey was wasted (as the veteran opined) in external lotions; but for a day or two I could only hang up the useless member, and make believe I had lost an arm at Gettysburg, and deserved well of a grateful republic. Since that time, I have had opportunity to study the yellow-jacket; and I know that, like other desperate characters who hold life cheap, he is to be respected and feared. He who would merely kill you may be a coward, after all, and you need not leave the country on his account; but he who hates you, and, in comparison with that passion, cares not whether you kill him or no, is dangerous. Avoid him if you can, treat him kindly when you may, smash him when you must; but be sure, that, nine times out of ten, he will first put dagger into you.

We strike into the well-trodden trail of the Indians, and frequently meet cavalcades of them returning, heavy-laden, from the great huckleberry-patches, where they collect their winter store. Others of them are spearing or netting salmon at the cascades of the Columbia and Des Chutes, and, with dried fish and fruit galore, they will pass a merry winter in their squalid manner. These fragmentary tribes of the Upper Columbia — Klikatats, and what not — are not so handsome as the Nez Percés, farther to the north-east; but there are now and then fine faces among them, — laughing-eyed young squaws, old men with judicial brows, straight, strong athletes, — and the children all promise a future beauty which privation, hardship, and disease too surely erase as they grow up. Was there a time when the Red Man roamed, &c., contented and happy, valiant and handsome, the perfect and worthy child of Nature? Show us the relics of former decent habitations, and good victuals, and we may, perchance, answer in the affirmative. But perpetually living out of doors, without clothes to speak of, and subsisting upon food in precarious supply and frequently of inferior quality, is not calculated to develop a high type of physical, any more than of mental manhood. If this doctrine be held to cast a slur upon Adam, who represents to us the state of savage innocence to which some people think we ought to return, I can only say that Adam's career was a disgraceful one. He had a better chance than the rest of us, and he ruined himself and his descendants by a piece of real Indian laziness and folly. Lolling about, and eating the spontaneous fruits of the earth, instead of tilling the garden with industry, is just his sin, and theirs. This copper-colored Adam, who was placed in the Eden of the New World, has mismanaged it in the same way. He and his dusky Eve have loitered and idled away the centuries, living carelessly upon the bounty of the passing time. Verily, by reason of family resemblance to Adam (and, for that matter, to Cain also), the Indians should be set down as a very early offshoot from the Eden stock, transplanted before the parent tree had begun its better growth.

"Too much preaching and philosophizing," says the Tourist, who is interested in the squaws and babies, and not at all in Adam. In deference to his wishes, I subside into silence and a trot. These Indians all talk Chinook, which is the most fascinating of tongues. Being the product of a deliberate agreement of men, — a compromise, it is said, between the Hudson's Bay Company's agents, the Jesuit missionaries, and the once powerful Chinook tribe, — it is, of course, superior to those misshapen dialects that spring up of themselves, no one knows how. From the French, Spanish, English, Indian, and Hawaiian, these wise etymologists took what was best in each, and the result comprises melody, force, and wondrous laconic expressiveness. It is none of your tame tongues, that can be spoken without gesture. Little boys declaiming in jargon could not possibly retain in nervous grasp the seams of their trouser-legs. One of the most frequent words is *kahkwa*, meaning "thus," or "like this," and invariably accompanied with pictorial illustration of movement or feature. Let us address this ancient chieftain, solemnly riding at the head of a long train of "cayuse" horses, laden with his household, his "traps," and his huckleberries: "*Klahowya sikhs?*" ("How dost thou, venerable sir?") "*kah mika klatawa?*" ("and whither journeyest?") "*Nika klatawa kopa Simcoe. Mika King George tilikum, Boston tilikum?*" ("I travel to the Simcoe Reservation. Are ye of King George's men, that is to say, Englishmen, — or of the Boston tribe, that is to say, Yankees?") "*Nesika Boston tilikum, King George cultus.*" ("We are Americans all, and regard King George with loathing and contempt.") "*Okook mika klootchman?*" we ask, ("Is you beauteous being thy bride?") "*Nawitka,*" ("Yes.") "*Siah kopa lamonti?*" ("Is it far to the mountains?" — *lamonti*, from the French *la montagne*.) "*Wake siah; wayhut hyas kloshe, okook sun; kah chilchil kahkwa tomolla keekwillie kahkwa; tomolla moosum kopa lamonti.*" ("Not far; good road to-day, steep; to-morrow, low and level, thus and thus; to-morrow night a camp at the mountain.") A very commonplace conversation, but full of music, as you will discover, if you read it aloud, Mademoiselle, with your sweet voice. But the Veteran is loping far ahead. Jargon has no charms for him: he has prattled too many years with these babes of the wood.

It is thirty-five miles from the mouth of the White Salmon to the ice-cave; and over this trail by which we travel the ice is "packed" upon the backs of mules and horses. We meet upon the road the loaded train. On each beast two sacks, each of which contained, at starting, a block of ice weighing, perhaps, two hundred pounds, but destined to melt away to half its original dimensions before it reaches the steamboat-landing. By this simple device, as the toilsome day wears on, the burden diminishes, and, while it grows lighter, distills refreshing coolness on the bearer. The dividends of the business would be larger, however, as the Portlander acutely remarks, if the ice were better packed at the cave. But this is a fair sample of the mining industry of the coast. Happy that enterprise, whereof the drippings *only* equal the savings!

The sun drops into the hazy west as we ride into a forest glade, and the Veteran exclaims, "Here she is!" We resolve upon an immediate preliminary examination of the cave, and subsequent supper and sleep. All that presented itself was an opening in the ground a dozen feet square, formed by the fall of a portion of the roof. We had passed, within a few hours, numerous openings of this kind, the mention of which I have omitted for artistic reasons. I would not fritter away the reader's interest in minor caverns on the way. The examination of several, however, qualifies me to give wise explanation of their nature.

These caves are channels in the basalt, through which the latest flows of melted matter passed. The phenomenon of a stream of lava walled and roofed with congealed material of the same character may be observed at almost any active volcano. I have seen it on the sides of Vesuvius during a quiet eruption. If the source of such a stream is suddenly choked, the lava will continue to flow for some distance, protected from rapid cooling by the crust above, and thus a portion of the channel will be left empty. It is not difficult to recognize this process in the basalt caves of Washington Territory. Their walls are covered with the traces of the departing fluid matter, and on their floors may be found masses of the congealed lava, still fibrous from its last vain effort to follow the current. It looks, my young friend, like that piece of abortive molasses candy which you threw away in despair, because it got so stiff and would not "pull." But whence the ice — that strange dweller in these homes of fire? That, also, you shall know.

Only a few of these caverns contain ice; and they are connected at both ends with the open air, by means of passages formed by the falling-in of the crust, or the fissuring of the rocks by frost, or, finally, by the gradual denudation of the surface, exposing the ancient channels themselves. The intense refrigerating airs of winter are thus allowed free passage. Alternately with these, the percolating waters of the surface find their way into the caves in such small quantities that they freeze, layer upon layer, solid from the bottom; and the store of ice thus accumulated thaws slowly during the summer. This summer thaw is retarded, not only by the covering which protects the ice from the direct rays of the sun, but also by the fact that the melting ice at one end of the cave, through which the summer draught enters, itself refrigerates the air, and maintains a freezing temperature at the other end. We noted in the main ice-cave, which we explored, a decided difference in the degrees of thaw at different points. This difference was due to the cause above mentioned; and I had the honor to determine it by sliding unintentionally down a glacial stalagmite, and observing practically the degree of moisture upon its surface. The popular report, that, as fast as ice is removed from the cave, it continually and at all seasons forms again, is without foundation. The amount of it in the cave is not very great, though as yet undetermined; and what there is, perpetually, though slowly, wastes away. The main body of ice has a level surface, indicating subterranean drainage at a certain point, above which water does not remain in the cave. There are a few stalactites, and still more numerous stalagmites, here and there. One of these is a superb, transparent hillock, rising nearly to the roof, and christened "the Iceberg." Here I took my slide.

The entrance used by the ice-miners is the opening in the roof already alluded to. At this point the channel turns at right angles, and this sharp turn left the roof with less support, so that it fell in. We followed the cave more than two hundred feet in one direction from this entrance, and perhaps five hundred in the other. The short arm of it contains most of the ice, and the long arm simply reaches out through fallen rocks and rubbish to daylight. The terminus of the cave in the other direction was reached by the Tourist, who, being a small man and an ambitious, hatcheted his way over the iceberg, and crawled out of sight into a fissure beyond, from the depths of which his voice was presently heard, announcing that it was "too tight a fit" for him to go farther. *Tableau:* Tourist in the hole, triumphant; Writer perched on the iceberg, curious, but cautious; portly Portlander, halfway to the entrance, resolving to have that hole made bigger when the hotel is built; and Veteran at the entrance, not caring a straw.

The dimensions of the cavern are not large. It does not exceed thirty feet in width, nor (at present, with the bottom full of ice and fallen fragments of basalt) twenty in height. Others in the neighborhood are larger, but do not contain so much ice. From the nature of their origin, it is not likely that any of them possess extraordinary dimensions, except in length. In this direction they extend for miles; though they can seldom be followed underground, without labor in removing rocks, &c., for more than a few hundred feet. It was in the present instance the indefatigable Tourist, who, with the docile Writer in his wake, made a second visit to Hades after supper, and, entering by the familiar chasm, found the new exit far to the south, and emerged thereby, to the great amazement of the party by the camp-fire, under whose unconscious feet they had passed, to re-appear in an unexpected quarter.

If you ever visit the cave, don't let the Veteran persuade you that it is necessary to ride two miles farther to camp, on account of water. There are pools of clear ice-water within it; and behind a tall pine, not far away, you will find two wooden troughs half sunk in the earth. One of them is very leaky; the other not so much. Let one of you stand at the bottom of the cave, and another lower from above the coffee-pot, made fast to a lariat. A third can run to and fro with the precious liquid; and in a few minutes you will have water for your horses in the trough. The Veteran will sit on a log, scornfully at first, but finally snort his approbation. At least, that was the order of operations on the present occasion.

The joys of camping out I do not undertake to describe. In this effeminate day, when people sit in their parlors and read about things, instead of doing them, thank goodness there is something left which can not be put into words! There is a period of perfect peace, when, rising at midnight, and putting a fresh log on the fire, one gazes placidly about upon his sleeping comrades, lights a pipe, and communes with himself, the dancing flame, and the solemn, silent forest. Interjected between the jollity of the evening meal and the business-like activity of breakfast, packing, and mounting, this midnight pipe of peace is like a whiff from another world. How ridiculously different from sitting up in bed, and lighting the gas!

Another thing which I omit is a description of fair St. Helen's and grand Mount Adams. How they accompany us with their eternal beauty all the way! How delightful is the change from the gloomy caves to the paradise that lies just beneath the edge of the melting snows on Mount Adams! There innumerable varieties of flowers bloom, even at this late season, — the whole Flora of the coast, — but dwarfed by their Alpine locality into forms of infinite delicacy, and, hovering among them, multitudes of humming-birds, who have gathered here to find again the blossoms of June, vanished long since from the South. Streams alive with trout (*hyiu tenas salmon*) and white goats on the snowy fields above, to tax the skill and daring of the more ambitious sportsman — I could give you a fine description of all these things; but I must stop here. And morally it is quite as well, for the smoke in the air prevented us from seeing Adams, or visiting the Paradise of Humming-birds — but which is, nevertheless, there; and so you will find out, when, next July, you add to your summer trip along the grand Columbia a charming three-days' excursion to the region I have faintly depicted.

THE ASCENT OF GRAY'S PEAK.[1]

THE ascent of the Rocky Mountains from the east begins so far away, that it is useless to include the whole of it in this brief sketch. Even at Omaha, one is nine hundred and sixty-six feet above sea-level; and, in traveling westward to Cheyenne, one trundles smoothly up hill, until, by imperceptible degrees, the altitude of six thousand and forty-one feet has been attained. The bugbear of the Rocky Mountains, and the way it vanishes when assailed, are a perpetual joke on mankind. One is amused, in the midst of the monotonous iteration of buffalo-grass and sky, by the recurrence of the reflection that this is the forbidden barrier between East and West, — about as much of a barrier as the hole in the fence through which one used, in comparative infancy, to kiss the little girl that lived next door, — a positive opportunity, an invitation, not a hindrance.

But if you think, fair reader, that the rest of the fence is like this easy gap in it, just come along with

[1] April, 1871.

me, and climb one of the pickets. We are going, two or three of us, to ascend Gray's Peak.

From Cheyenne to Denver is a ride over the Plains of about a hundred and ten miles. The new railroad is excellently built and stocked. The view from the car-window is enlivened by glimpses of prairie-dogs erect on stern at the doors of their burrows, and now and then an owl blinking in the sun. The dogs and owls do live together — in the proportion of a great many dogs to one owl: wisdom is in the minority in this world. But don't you believe that story about the rattlesnakes being members of the same happy families. As far as I can find out, the snakes inhabit the holes, as the first of them may have lived in Eden, after the ejection of the original tenants. Believe what good you choose about all other branches of creation, but never you let up on snakes: that way lies heresy.

There are antelopes too, — charming compounds of timidity and curiosity, — their slender legs carrying them swiftly away as the train approaches, and their slender noses, with skillful leverage, whirling them about to sniff and stare. But we do not need these petty distractions; for, lo! — vision denied till now through all the weary way — the great mountains themselves now loom up, silent and majestic on the west, and accompany us, hour after hour, with their shining crests, and purple cañons, and floating wreaths of cloud. The sun sets behind them, and their glories vanish in a cold, gray monotone. You should see them at sunrise, if you would learn their infinite beauty. Then the — but this won't do: we have got to climb Gray's Peak, and we are using up all the adjectives beforehand. That's Gray's Peak yonder; and that other, close by, is Irwin's. Away to the north is Long's; and terminating our view of the range to the south is Pike's, grandest in outline of them all. This view of two hundred miles of the Rocky Mountains in one picture, from the Plains by Denver, is not surpassed in the world. The Alps seen from the top of Milan Cathedral are lovely, but too faint and far. There is a place on the old road from Dalles City to Cañon City in Oregon, where a similar panoramic view of the Cascade Range may be obtained, including Shasta, Jefferson, The Sisters, Hood, St. Helena, Adams, and even (to a good eye, favored with a clear day, a first-rate glass, and a fine imagination) Baker, and Rainier. That view is equal to this; but it is a great deal harder to reach. So, considering all things, we may decide that the display of the mountains before Denver is the finest thing of the kind ever provided by Nature, and developed by railroads.

This thrifty settlement, by the way, is the new colony of Greeley. Two hundred houses already, and not a solitary one last spring. The inhabitants all have more or less capital, and so they will escape the poverty-stricken children of most pioneer settlements. There are only one or two Democrats in town, — not enough to keep the Republican party from splitting. And there are no liquor-stores at all, — a miracle in these parts. Is it partially accounted for by the very near neighborhood of Evans (only a couple of miles away), formerly a temporary terminus of the railroad, and a very busy place, where now there is scarcely any thing left but saloons and bars? Let us hope that the Greeleyites will let Evans alone.

But here we are at Denver, a pretty town, more substantially built than any other of the interior, not even excepting Salt Lake. Denver has three railroads already, — the Denver Pacific to Cheyenne, the Kansas Pacific to Kansas City and St. Louis, and the Colorado Pacific to Golden City, — all shortened, to save the valuable time of hotel clerks and runners, to the D. P., the K. P., and the C. P. Remember, moreover, that, if you take the D. P., you must be going to Cheyenne to connect with the U. P.: so mind your P's and cues, or you'll lose your baggage.

The Colorado Pacific, with sublime audacity, strikes straight at the heart of the mountains What it has to do with the ocean whence it borrows half its name, can only be seen by continuing the line of the road through a dozen or more of the highest ranges in the country. This process is easy on a map with a lead-pencil; but drawing a line is not drawing a train. However, there is inspiration in names, and nobody knows what may happen. A few years ago any Pacific railroad was chimerical: a few years hence all of them may be achieved and trite, and we may be laughing at the Kamtschatka Baltic, or the Cape of Good Hope Mediterranean, or the Patagonia Arctic.

Having had our joke, let us take our tickets. Fifteen miles, or thereabout, is the distance to Golden City, the present terminus of the railroad. The route winds among grassy foothills capped with basalt, that seem to be a compromise between rugged mountain and rolling plain. Golden is nestled among them, — a thriving, ambitious town, endowed with fire-clay, coal-mines, and a fine seminary. A territorial school of mines is about to be established here; possibly the students will find the locality more agreeable, but less profitable, than Georgetown or Central, where the arts of mining and metallurgy are extensively illustrated in practice.

Not desiring to visit Central at present, we will cross over from Golden to the main stage-road for Georgetown. The excellent coaches of the Colorado Stage Company bear us to Idaho City, and hence up the long, magnificent Virginia Cañon to Georgetown.

Idaho (let us drop the " City : " most of these mountain towns were founded for metropolitan purposes, and their high-sounding titles now have a ring of disappointment; so that the inhabitants save themselves both time and mortification by dropping the suggestive appendix: hence Denver, Golden, Central, Virginia, Ruby, Empire, Diamond, Star, and what not; hence, also, Idaho) is picturesquely situated at the meeting of two or three cañons, the main one being that of Clear Creek. Certain hot-springs give the town a permanent importance as a watering-place: and numerous mines in the neigborhood bestow upon it the flickering reflections of their fluctuating prosperity. The ten miles of Clear Creek Cañon that lie between this and Georgetown are full of fine rock scenery, not unlike portions of the Via Mala in Switzerland, though here the snowy peaks are not in view. People say, moreover, that the legendary and historic charms which add so much to the attractions of Nature in foreign lands are wanting in our own; but that is a mistake. If you don't believe it, talk to the driver. The guide told you, somewhere in the Alps, did he? of a peasant who found the treasures of the mountain-elves, and when he went to look for them again, with a party of friends to carry them away, lo! there was nothing but barren rock. Bless you, that happens here every day! Up yonder, a thousand feet over your head, is a white rock. That is the outcrop of the Salamander Ledge. The man that owned it knew it was the mother-lode of the Rocky Mountains; the geologist who examined it was sure it was the real "igneous fatuous" rock, and no mistake; and the company that bought it proposed to pay the national debt, after satiating their stockholders. But there never was a pound of ore discovered in it, except the specimens that went East, and there is a touch of the legendary in them even. Beat that story in the Alps, if you can.

They talk, too, about ruined castles, stately old rookery on a hill, desolate cloister in the valley, knight went to Palestine in olden days, villain waylaid knight, began suit to lady, rascally priest mixed up in the business, and so on. Not a bit more pathetic than the history of yonder magnificent pile, the Megatherium Mill, with its pristine splendor, knights and ladies (pardon me, Madam, for alluding to them), its suits and battles, its final abandonment and present desolation. The lively dwelling-house beyond is a monastery now, and a monk in red flannel shirt and long beard smokes a pipe there.

Ruined aqueducts of the Campagna? We can match them too. Look at these flumes and ditches, and grim, toothless wheels, sported by the current they once controlled! See the heaps of boulders, every one of which has been lifted by zealous hands, if perchance the philosopher's stone might lie beneath. Yes, the romance of the past is here. These wild scenes are clothed, as truly as those of the elder world, with the ambitions, hopes, disappointments, and tragedies of the human heart.

But all around us here is the life and busy industry of the present. Fortunes are carved out of these rocks; and Clear Creek Cañon discharges to the wide plains and the wider world its steady stream of wealth. Of course, I don't mean to say this is romantic. I throw in the remark merely for the information of capitalists, and to satisfy my conscience, which might otherwise be quickened unpleasantly by some justice-loving citizen of Colorado, who would fire a revolver or a leading article at me to remind me that the territory is by no means dead yet.

Here is Georgetown, imbosomed in the mountains which overshadow it on every side, and leave it only space enough to be comfortable and beautiful. It is, indeed, a lovely site, and doubly so by comparison with the awkwardness of Central, squeezed into its three or four precipitous cañons as one rubs putty in a crack. Georgetown possesses, however, what Central doesn't even claim, — a good hotel. On the other hand, — let us be just, and *then* fear not, — the mines about Central produce a great deal more money at this time; the achievements of the districts around Georgetown being but respectable at present, and magnificent in future.

Perhaps you think we are coming but slowly to Gray's Peak. Not so. While I have beguiled the way with gossip, we have steadily ascended, until now we are some nine thousand feet above the sea. You wouldn't have a man begin to climb a mountain at nine thousand feet, and call that the outset? Reflect, moreover, that I had a clear right to begin at the Atlantic Ocean. Where should we be now in that case? Certainly not out of the clutches of Chicago. Sleep in peace this night: to-morrow's sunrise will see us far on our way.

"To-morrow's sunrise" is a phrase carefully chosen;

for the sun makes no haste to rise in these deep cañons. We may even, on our winding route, enjoy half a dozen sunrises, plunging again, after each one, into the chill shadows of last night. But gloriously tipped with gold are the crest-ridges, and steadily the luster crawls down the steep rock-faces, until at last the glowing day is everywhere, save in those profound coverts where the cold, clear springs are hidden under tufted mosses and closely-twined arms of Dryads, and in the subterranean recesses of shaft, or tunnel, or stope, where the swart miner swings the sledge in perpetual midnight.

Mounted on the active, sure-footed horses of this region (which have better endurance than the coursers of the plains, as the Denver boys found out when they bet their money at the Georgetown races), we follow the wagon-road up the cañon of the north fork of the middle branch, or the middle fork of the south branch, — or something to that effect, — of South Clear Creek. The stream was once well named. They say one could count the trout in its waters — only they were too many to be counted. But sluices and tailings have long ago corrupted its lower course. Only up here towards its source is it still worthy, in some degree, of its pretty title. The turnpike follows it patiently, under many difficulties, now clinging along a steep bluff far above it, now crossing it by a rustic bridge, now peacefully enjoying for a season its close company through a bit of fertile or gravelly bottomland. The mountains crowd us all they can, and now and then they seem to have cornered us entirely. Just above Georgetown there is apparently no way out of the *cul-de-sac* into which they have driven our brave little creek; but a way there is, and through it Clear Creek leaps into Georgetown. Of course the gap is called the Devil's Gate, or something similarly diabolical. It is the Western way to clap the infernalest names on the heavenliest places, flying, in such cases as this, moreover, in the face of Scripture, which informs us that the Devil's gate is not narrow, but broad and easy.

The mountain-sides are still covered with timber, though sadly scarred by great fires which the recklessness of the inhabitants occasions or permits. The straight, dead pines, first charred and afterwards bleached, bristle like gray porcupine-quills on the back of the range. In the more accessible places wood-cutters are at work, felling the dry timber, and shooting it down the steep precipices to the valley. All along the base of the mountains are the mouths of inchoate tunnels, reminding us of those curious organisms that begin with a mouth only, and develop their bowels afterward. High above, sometimes fifteen hundred feet over the stream, are dumps and windlasses, showing where the silver-veins have been found. So many promising veins have been discovered on these bare summits, that it is almost a maxim with some of the prospectors that, —

> "A good silver-mine
> Is above timber-line
> Ten times out of nine."

But let us drop the subject. That way lies science.

At Brownsville, three miles distant from Georgetown, are the Brown and Terrible Mines, and the smelting-works of the former company. The mines are situated up a steep, rocky gulch, above the Brown works, the Brown Mine being uppermost, and the Terrible between. The ore extracted from the Brown is brought down on an aerial tramway, the rails of which are tightly-stretched wire-cables; and in this way the Brown transportation goes on through the air, over the heads of the Terrible people. The smoke and fumes from the smelting-works float up the cañon for a long distance, and supply the cloud hitherto lacking in this morning's spotless sky.

Three miles farther, through the constantly narrowing and rising valley, bring us to the settlement and the handsome mill of the Baker Company. It is this company to which we are indebted for the good road we have traveled thus far: and indeed the blessing is not yet exhausted; for the company's mine is not far from the summit of Gray's Peak, and the company's teams have made a capital wagon-road up to the mines.

At this point we leave Clear Creek, and follow up a tributary known as Kelso. The road now mounts more steeply. The pines and quaking-asps, dwarfed somewhat in stature, come close to us as we ride, as though they were lonesome, and huddled along the road to catch a social glance or word from a passing traveler. The birds and squirrels, so plenty a mile below, suddenly cease to be seen or heard. The peculiar stillness of the upper air makes itself felt. Presently we have emerged from the last belt of timber, and are alone with heaven.

No, not yet! Hundreds of feet still above us, on the side of Kelso Mountain, are the buildings of the Baker Mine. A shanty may mean any thing; but a house with a chimney is a sign of permanent habitation. At that warning finger, Solitude gets up and goes. Nevertheless, barring the Baker Mine, the scene is grand as Nature before the age of man. On the right, Kelso Mountain turns to us a rounded, conical form, grass-clad. On the left, McClellan Mountain presents a circling ridge; the face turned toward us being as steep and rugged as it can be, and not fall over. Whoever has ascended Vesuvius, and remembers how the central cone arises from within the surrounding precipices of a former crater, will comprehend the general position of the parts of this wild scene. But these rocks are not volcanic. The farther side of McClellan is sloping, like this side of Kelso; and the farther side of Kelso is rough and perpendicular, like this side of McClellan; and the ridge of McClellan does not completely surround Kelso, but at its farther end soars up into two peaks, and there stops.

These two peaks are Gray's and Irwin's; and, as we journey, they come into full near view from behind the head of Kelso.

I am glad enough that the scene is not volcanic. This gray granite, or gneiss, has far greater variety and beauty of form, and gives us delicate shadows. Though it may lack the imperial purples of trachytes and tufas seen in the distance, it does not offer us their horrid blackness seen near by. Besides, there are dainty grasses and blossoms that sometimes hang by one hand from clefts in the granite, and swing in the wind. Yosemite, Smoky Valley, and Gray's Peak, — let the lava people, with their Snake Cañons, Shoshone Falls, and gloomy Dalles, match this granite trio if they can!

It is lucky that our path doesn't lie up that face of McClellan Mountain. Lie? It couldn't: it would have to stand. No mortal could climb there without wings. But what is that a thousand feet up the cliff? A house — ye gods! a boarding-house! The glass shows us fragments of a zigzag trail, interspersed with ladders where the precipices are otherwise impassable. Now we see, at the foot of the cliff, another house, and between the two, fine lines, like a spider's web, stretched through a thousand feet of air. That is the somewhat celebrated Stevens Mine. The men, lumber, provisions, &c., are all carried up, and the ore is all brought down, by means of one of the ingenious wire-tramways now becoming common in

Colorado. How the mine was ever discovered, I can not say: somebody must have "lit on it."

The summit is close before us now, glistening with patches of snow. On the neck between Gray and Irwin, there is a regular turnover collar of a drift. It looks small enough here; but you couldn't pass it without a twenty-foot tunnel in the snow. There's not much life up here, — scarcely even a mountain-goat or a snow-quail for a six-hundred-dollar breakfast. Bill, here, will tell you that story: he hasn't opened his mouth the whole way.

"Well, 'tain't much of a story; but it gives the Georgetown boys the deadwood on Dick Irwin and me, and they hain't let up on us yet, nor wont s'long's they kin git anybody to swop lies with 'em. However, this yer's no lie. Ye see Dick and me — that thar mountain was named after Dick; that is to say, these two was ary one Irwin's Peak, and whichary wasn't Irwin's was Gray's, and nobody knowed. Gray, he was a great weed-sharp down East somewhar, and he gin so many names to this yer bunch-grass and stuff, that they thought they'd gin his name to the highest peak, though I don't see it myself. So these scientific fellers kept a-comin' up here, and a-measurin', and they couldn't agree. Some on 'em biled water on the top, and some on 'em friz mercury; but they couldn't agree. So at last a lot on 'em fresh from college camped out all night right on the top of Gray's, and took observations, you bet! every five minutes; and when *they* come down there wasn't no manner of doubt in *their* minds but what Gray's was the highest peak in the whole fandango. So Dick he come down like a gentleman, and took the next best himself. Well, Dick and me was out huntin', and looking up blossom-quartz around yer, and we raised one of these yer white snow-quails, and I found the nest with six eggs into it. So says I to Dick, ' You jest hold on, an' we'll have a reg'lar Delmonico sockdologer.' And we fried them there eggs, and eat 'em; and Dick said, Bust his crust, if he'd ever had a breakfast set so comfortable-like as that one did. ' All we want,' says Dick, ' is a drop of whisky to wash it down.' So we went down to Bakerville, and was a-settin' round in the bar-room as sociable as you please, spittin' on the stove, when Dick happened to mention them snow-quails' eggs; and a long, slab-sided, scientific son of a gun, with spectacles, riz up like a derrick, and says he, 'My friend, the Smithsonian Institution has offered a reward of one hundred dollars for a single specimen of the snow-quail's egg.' Most anybody would 'a' stopped to swear, and have a drink on that; but it never was nothin' but an idee and a start with Dick Irwin. When he thought of a thing, he was goin' to do it sure; and this time he made just two jumps out of doors, and moseyed up the mountain, with his rifle. Afore we saw him agin, he had been away down on the Grand, and all through the Snowy and the Wasatch. Then we heerd on him in the

Middle Park; and one day he walked over the range, and into the bar-room at Bakerville, as if nothin' had happened; and says he, 'Boys, that six-hundred-dollar breakfast has used up the last snow-quail's egg in the whole dam Rockies. What'll ye take?'"

Not so well told, Bill, as when first you reeled it off to me under the shadow of McClellan. However, this expurgated version, though not so good for your reputation as a *raconteur*, is doubtless better for your soul.

We have reclined on a sunny bit of grass, letting our horses nibble their luncheon while we disposed of our own, Bill's employment as a story-teller serving to keep him down to a fair share of the sandwiches and sardines. Now let us scale the final peak. It looks but a short distance, yet it is a good hour's work. You need not walk, however: the horses are used to it.

The peak seems to be formed of loose fragments of rock, piled up in confusion How did they get here? They didn't get here: they were here always. This heap of stones is the effect of ages of frost and snow and wind upon the once solid rock. At our left, as we ascend, stands a solitary crag, which has not yet quite yielded, nor toppled into ruins, but is seamed and cracked through and through.

No extensive prospect from here. It is one of the advantages of this route, that we mount gradually, and without great trouble, yet do not have the final glory of the view from the summit wasted upon us in driblets by the way. McClellan and Gray and Irwin still rise solidly between us and the land of promise, into which we shall presently gaze. There are snow-drifts here and there, but not enough to trouble us. The trail goes back and forward, winding sharply among the rocks. We have not yet risen above all life. There are tracks of light-footed animals in the snow; and yonder, as I live! there is one more mine. Yes, the Atlantic and Pacific Lode sits astride the backbone of the continent; and the enthusiastic discoverer, sure of having found at last the argentiferous heart of the continent, has put down a shaft exactly on the divide. Pity that a location so admirable for drainage and ventilation should have to be abandoned "for lack of capital"! We must wait for the C. P. to come this way.

But, the last turn and the last snowdrift being passed, we stand at last on the summit of Gray's Peak. It is a place for deep breaths of delight and admiration, but not for words, at least not until, the first ecstasy of silence being passed, the inevitable member of the party who carries the opera-glass, and who knows all the geography of the scene, begins to dispense his information. Never mind him. He is a good fellow; but he has been here before, and you have not. Hear what he has to say, and then sit on a rock beyond ear-shot, and look for yourself.

Southward, the crowding summits of the range,

intersected by the deep cañons of the Platte and its tributaries, and, beyond all, Pike's Peak, superb in the sun.

Westward, sweeping the circle from the south, the South and Middle Parks, pieces of the plains, caught and half-lifted by the mountains, in the midst of which their broad, fair surfaces lie imbosomed; the dark, tiny cañons of the Blue and other streams, that hasten to join the great south-western system of waters. One of them is full of clinging smoke; the woods are a-fire for miles. Far beyond the Parks is the Snowy Range, and the lofty peak of Mount Lincoln. Down in this labyrinth of glades, cliffs, and gorges, emerald lakes and rushing streams, there are human beings living and laboring, digging and sluicing, blasting and crushing, scalping or being scalped — for the Arraphoes make a dash at the Utes or the whites, now and then, in the Middle Park — but we reck nothing of it all. We might imagine ourselves to be the first who were looking on the fair expanse, but for this piece of "The New-York Herald," and this old sardine-box, left by a former party, and the minute cluster of dots in one of those far cañons, which closer inspection reveals to be the town of Montezuma.

Northward, infinite variety of battlements, spires, domes, and whatever other thing you choose to name, by way of dwarfing the sublimity you cannot describe; innumerable vistas and half-revelations; Irwin's Peak in the foreground, looming up on a level with us, so near, apparently, that one might throw a stone to its lone flagstaff and skeleton of a tent; Long's Peak closing the view in the distance, brown and cloud-hung.

Eastward, another turn of the marvelous kaleidoscope, and a new combination of the endless beauties of outline, tint, and shade; and beyond all ending and blending in the illimitable sky, the vast ocean of the Plains.

Upward, the empty heavens, speaking unutterable things; and everywhere the thin, pure, sweet mountain-air, which one rather drinks than breathes, feeling the while that intoxicating combination of inspiring stimulus and delicious languor which nothing else bestows.

It takes a good while to go up to Gray's Peak; but mark how short a tale shall put you down. A climb for descending the steep summit, leading the horses, — a brisk ride, with gallops interspersed, down the valley, through deepening twilight — and at last, beneath the glamour of a full white moon — Georgetown — Denver, C. P. R. R.

www.ingramcontent.com/pod-product-compliance
Lightning Source LLC
Chambersburg PA
CBHW020809230426
43666CB00007B/932